How To Get More Appliance Repair Leads Online & Turn Them Into Paying Customers!

Marlon Thomas

Copyright © 2019 **Marlon Thomas**

All rights reserved. No part of this book may be reproduced or transmitted in any form or by any means without the written permission of the author.

ISBN-13: 978-179621061-3

Contents

Introduction 1

Chapter 1 - Why Most Appliance Repair Businesses Struggle To Get A Consistent Flow Of Leads 6

Chapter 2 - The Shift In Marketing 10

Chapter 3 - Feel Like A Victim Of Advertising? 14

Chapter 4 - Your Ideal Customer Is Online, Are You? 17

Chapter 5 - How To Get Your Appliance Repair Company Ranked On Page One Using Google Maps 19

Chapter 6 - Increase Your Appliance Repair Leads With Paid Search 38

Chapter 7 – The SEO Formula 55

Chapter 8 - Why You Should Consider Yelp For Appliance Repair Leads 76

Chapter 9 - How To Get Yelp Working For Your Business 78

Chapter 10 - Add Craigslist To Your Marketing Plan 81

Chapter 11 – Pay Per Lead And NOT Per Click With Google's Local Service Ads 83

Chapter 12 – Convert MORE Of Your Website's Visitors Into Callers! 101

Chapter 13 - How Much Your Leads Are Really Worth? 114

Chapter 14 - Do You know the "True" Cost Of Your Leads? 118

Chapter 15 - Do You Know Where Your Appliance Repair Leads Are Coming From? 124

APPENDICES 129

The Ultimate Appliance Repair ONLINE MARKETING CHECKLIST! 130

More FREE Stuff! 134

About the Author 140

Introduction

Welcome To Today's Economy:

The old economy is gone, never to be seen again.

Although history has a way of repeating itself, when it comes to things like fashion, the way to market an appliance repair company 10 or 20 years ago, is never coming back.

Now don't get me wrong, there are certain things like offering excellent customer service that will never go away and will still be around 20 years from now because that is a reliable time-honored business strategy.

Good customer service is probably more important now than ever, but it now needs to be combined with new school, more disciplined and sophisticated marketing methods.

The new economy has been created by advancement in technologies that make consumers lives easier and as the owner of an appliance repair company you need to synchronize these realities with the psychology of today's consumers.

It's not like we didn't see these changes coming....

Some examples of things coming, where Starbucks popping up on what seems like every street corner. Credit got easy as banks relaxed their lending guidelines like never before, so many consumers started to use their homes as ATM machines....

Let's discuss how Today's economy and the impact on local appliance repair companies:

1. The consumer has all the power, and they know all too well that they have it.
2. Consumers no longer want "ordinary" as they have higher expectations now and with very little barrier

to entry for someone to start an appliance repair business, the consumer knows they have choices and a lot of them.

3. Before hiring an appliance repair company, they want proof that you can earn their trust. With a large number of review sites like Yelp, you better believe they are reading reviews before picking up that phone.
4. You must design your business around their schedule if you want to expand into a big business, don't want to work after 5 or on weekends? That's ok, they will find an appliance repair company that will, and they will get this accomplished in a matter of minutes with the help of search engines like Google.

Today's consumers are incredibly demanding, and appliance repair companies that want to succeed will not be given customers, but instead, they have to earn their business. Your appliance repair company needs an edge over the competition, simply put.... you must be better.

In this book, I want to show you how to market your appliance repair business successfully, with online marketing strategies. For some of you, all this information may be new to you. If that is you, don't worry, as I will be holding your hand along the way.

Once you have completed reading this book you will have a much better understanding of the appliance repair online marketing arena.

Finding new customers can be one of the day to day challenges that most appliance repair company owners face, and I am sure you would agree with me on that.

For others, the problem is not finding new customers, but instead it's finding them in a cost-effective manner and or retaining the customers they already have.

These are the questions that are top of mind for most local appliance repair business owners in today's economy!

If you are NOT getting enough new customers to call your company for new service calls, or if you are simply not bringing in enough revenue for your business right now ... Then you have to do yourself a favor, take some time out of your busy day, get your favorite beverage to drink and read this book thoroughly.

Your perception of marketing in general will be forever changed. And that's a good thing because things are constantly evolving.

The information you are about to read on the next few pages may well be what you have been looking for, the missing piece to the **online marketing puzzle**.

These are tested and proven business building strategies that we implement to get our existing clients hundreds of leads each month and they are based on real-life examples case studies like:

Ron Stetz, owner of Ron's Appliance in Fort Lauderdale Florida, a 40+ year appliance repair technician and business owner. Stetz recently told me:

I do many types of advertising for appliance repair leads. One of the marketing companies that I work with and is my best source of jobs, is The Appliance Experts. Marlon the owner is very intelligent, calm and understanding and we work well together.

I have recently recommended his services to my son in New Jersey who also owns an appliance repair business. I have worked with Marlon for over 3 years, and I hope to continue for a long long time.

Have you ever thought about the following?

- What it would be like to have your appliance repair company's website show up at the top of Google and the other search engines when consumers in your local service area are looking to hire an appliance repair company?
- To get a flood of leads calling your service company regularly, that found your company online?
- To know that you are taking full advantage of online marketing to get maximum exposure, branding, leads, and profits?
- What it would mean to you if you could double your profits?
- How better you would rest at night knowing that you had a lead generation system in place to keep your techs consistently busy?

All the above is what I want for you to accomplish by taking time to read this book.

What You'll Find Inside:

- Marketing fundamentals – so that you can have a solid foundation to build on.
- A roadmap showing you which online marketing strategies you should be focusing on to grow your appliance repair business.
- How to get page one rankings for your appliance repair business for the most important appliance repair keywords in your local service area.
- Want to rank in Google Maps? We'll give you a proven strategy to get your listing to show up in the top 3 spots.
- How to use social media to get more referrals and repeat business from your existing customers.

Again, all this information is based on real world, in the trenches experience, from other appliance repair companies just like yours.

Yes, I am in the appliance repair lead generation business, and I would obviously love the opportunity to partner with you and sell you leads.

But that isn't why I wrote this book, so no there is no sales pitch, so please don't expect one.

Instead, I wrote this book so that I could share with you some of our best lead generation strategies and information that you can implement within your appliance repair business to get more leads from the internet.

That's the goal of this book and it's not a sales presentation.

The best way to use this book is to read the entire book, find all of the sections that apply to you, then review those sections and start implementing the material.

To finding more customers and to your future business success!

Marlon

Chapter 1 - Why Most Appliance Repair Businesses Struggle To Get A Consistent Flow Of Leads

Here's THE HONEST TRUTH:

Majority of local appliance service company owners have no clue about how to advertise their repair business and *ATTRACT NEW CUSTOMERS*! In today's economy....

I know you already have some type of success getting customers, so don't misunderstand what I am saying.

But let's just say I gave you a challenge?

To get 10 new customers in the next 5 days... *can you pinpoint an exact strategy for doing this???*

My suspicion is that the majority of company owners reading this book will answer **NO** ...

So how do most appliance repair companies find their existing customers?

Well ... Most past and existing customers probably came from some sort of word-of-mouth advertising ... Am I right?

The formula is simple, do a good job to make your customers happy, and they will refer you to their friends and family.

But maybe you have also done some old school marketing to get new customers running Yellow Page Ads, Newspaper Ads or even networking events, etc. All of these advertising methods still work to some extent... but how effective would these sources be to guarantee you 10 new customers in the next 5 days?

I'm sure you will agree, that none the sources we just discussed are that predictable and I know for a fact not even the advertising reps could guarantee you a specific number of clients in such short time frame.

Of course, I am assuming you want to grow your business, which is why you are reading this book?

Most of the appliance repair company owners and managers that I speak to will tell me that the only way they know of to go out and get new customers is to spend MORE money on advertising and that is because that's all they have been told over the years from the traditional advertising reps.

It may be that you pay for bigger and better-designed ads in the Yellow Pages, buy a half page or full page ad in the local paper instead of doing classified ads, possibly buying more airtime during the peak drive time on your local radio station ... all of these are supposedly designed to get your phone ringing off the hook with new customers. But the truth is, these rarely perform in that way.

Depending on how you talk to, you will find different solutions, which is what makes appliance repair advertising so confusing. Do any of these solutions sound familiar:

- Companies that sell websites will blame that fact that you are not getting customers because of the website you currently have and will say you need a new website.
- The Yellow Pages reps will tell you that you need to be on their new Online Yellow Pages, along with paying for bigger Ads.
- Branding experts will say, yes, and you can probably guess it, the positioning and branding of your service company is the problem.

Make you wonder. Are they really trying to help you grow your business, are they really on your side?

There are 2 big problems with traditional advertising:

- Costs lot of money to implement and rarely gets the results you want.
- Make a mistake and you are stuck with your mistakes for the entire campaign.

Now, what about your website?

You've got one, right? If you don't, we'll talk later how to get a free or low-cost solution.

Do you know when was the last time you got a new customer from your website?

A website done correctly should be your virtual employee working for you 24/7/365.
If your website is not bringing in new customers, don't feel bad, it's really not your fault, while websites are a powerful marketing tool, statistics show that 1 in 20 websites are not set-up to bring in new customers!

I personally have experienced all these frustrations! I wanted to grow my company and thought many advertising reps were my allies, so I relied on them for the best advice, they told me to spend more money, so I spent it. At that point in my life, I lacked something fundamental as a business owner.... The right sales & marketing strategy to get a constant flow of new customers for my business ...

I got to a point where I was just Fed up with the LACK OF RESULTS!

My frustrations drove me to figure out for myself what the missing piece was from my current marketing! I studied every marketing book and course I could get my hands on. Eventually, I figured it out....

You see... Local appliance repair businesses are starting to become aware of the fact that mobile devices and the internet have changed the way consumers want to be marketed to and how business owners advertise to get in front of today's consumers when their appliances are broken.

Why are appliance repair companies changing their advertising strategy?

Simple.... With today's online media, the return on investment is much higher.

Consumers don't use or respond to traditional advertising strategies the way they use to, they have become immune to them.

Do you still have a yellow page directory at home?

Or

Like most of us consumers, you just throw it in the recycle bin when you received it?

It's amazing how small today's yellow page directories are compared to the '80s and '90s

Owners of appliance repair companies that are still using these outdated forms of marketing are throwing away good money at ineffective marketing.

Chapter 2 - The Shift In Marketing

Do you know something that the following industries actually have in common?

I'm talking about train or locomotive, newspaper or publishing, and the manufacturing industries.

And no, that's not a trick question…. give up?

Drum roll please…

Each of those industries at least failed to adjust to a massive shift…. that simply are making them obsolete. The thing is they had an opportunity to take advantage of it but didn't, and now they are trying to play catch up.

This is how it all happened…

Newspaper and generally the print media are a dying industry…. thanks to the internet and popular electronic readers such as the nook kindle and of course the iPad.

Trains and the locomotives have been replaced too….by cars and trucks.

Offshore outsourcing to developing countries is replacing the manufacturing industry.

This is a well-documented HISTORY…. and as we all know HISTORY never lies.

Now let's just look at another example, taking place closer to home. When you think of the growing presence of companies like the Wal-Mart, Amazon & Home Depot, you can't fail to notice how they have led to the shutdown of most "mom and pop" traditional stores. It's not possible for them to compete with these 800lb gorillas.

Do you know anyone who doesn't use a cell phone nowadays?

What happened to the home phones?

Landlines and all the pay phones that littered our streets have now become extinct.

Cable has almost destroyed the Network TV, and now Netflix, Redbox and other sites like Hulu is threatening to destroy cable.

Remember Blockbuster Video stores, Redbox and Netflix forced them out of business.

Think of a bag of Salad that now can outsell LETTUCE.

GPS systems already replaced the maps on paper forever. And now you can't buy a smartphone that doesn't come with a GPS application for free.

Uber is taking over the Taxi industry; I expect the big players like Yellow Cab will soon be filing bankruptcy. And the crazy thing is Uber doesn't even own the cars.

What about Airbnb, they are threatening the hotel industry, they already have more bookings per year than the major hotel chains and they do not own any real estate.

Horses were replaced by cars, newspapers crushed by radio, TV beat the radio.... I could go on and on, but I am sure you get the picture.

Now imagine that happening to your appliance repair business?

That is already happening to appliance repair businesses that have stuck to the old ways of marketing through traditional media like newspapers, postcards, yellow pages and space ads. If you continue doing like them.... then the competition can easily replace you....

It is the NATURAL path for business development.

The Marketing Paradigm has already shifted.... more consumers have switched to the use of online media whenever they need to research about products or services ....and they do it all the time before making their buying decision.

Some people repeatedly say that only young people are using online technologies to do shopping.... but that's a myth.

Fact: Online technologies have become the most popular way of shopping for the majority of consumers of all ages. Did you know that senior citizens are the fastest growing Facebook user group?

When I talk of a shift in the Marketing Paradigm, what exactly do I mean?

What that simply means is that marketing no longer works as a one-way communication channel.... but instead has now become a multi-channel conversation. What used to happen in the past relied on one-way communications that was almost exclusively broadcasted over traditional mass media such as newspapers, radio, TV and also the Yellow Pages distributed door-to-door.

Initially, when companies started marketing online, they were just building websites and then sending out emails to their customers; — But the problem with this strategy of marketing is that it was still one-way communication.

However, in recent years after the emergence of Web 2.0, which includes social media, the consumers started to control communication.

What then should this mean for local appliance repair businesses?

Consumers researching appliance service companies to fix their appliances will now depend more on what they learn from online communities.

These are consumer communities established across various online media and ask each other for experiences, opinions, and referrals or recommendations. Whether online or even offline, social media such as Facebook, Twitter, Yelp and similar platforms, now represent the new form of "word-of-mouth" and consumers trust it.

The internet initially became popular because it improved communication and connected people to share information.

Soon large corporations were able to tap into the power that the internet brought, making a serious impact on their growth of sales numbers and acquisition of customers. Every major corporation had to follow suit and did their best to establish an online presence.

Owners of small businesses thought that only large companies could manage to make proper use of the internet because they could afford huge budgets for advertising.

Well, today's technology has leveled the playing field, and I happily report that things have changed. Your small or medium sized appliance repair company now has a chance to market using the internet and can compete with the giants. You can even do internet marketing with a much smaller budget.

However, it's absolutely important to use the right marketing strategies if you want to come out successful.

Chapter 3 - Feel Like A Victim Of Advertising?

When most appliance repair company owners start advertising, they look around at what their competition is doing to find new customers and start doing the same things.

Seems logical, doesn't it?

The problem with that approach is they never really know whether or not those forms of advertising are actually working and the crazy thing is if you were to ask most of those appliance repair company owners if those forms of advertising are working, most wouldn't have a clue, because they don't track it.

I'm sure you have had advertising agencies bombarding you with ads telling you:

"You need to get your name out there so when people think of appliance repair they will call you."

This is the advertising salesperson's standard sales pitch.

They want you to put your company on the following:
- Television
- Radio
- Shopping Carts
- Billboards
- Yellow Pages
- Newspapers
- Placemats
- Websites

The list goes on and on.

Most of us small business owners fall into this trap, because it seems logical, I know I did. The only problem is these forms of advertising don't work as well as they use to.

When I confronted these advertising representatives, I quickly realized that they might get confronted about how effective their recommendations are, because they all seem to have a "canned" reply.

"You've got to give it time."

Or

"Keep running it and you will get responses."

Give me a break!

The only people benefit in these types of scenarios is the advertising agency and the ad rep. Think about this for a minute. If they really had a clue about how effectively advertise and market, would they really be selling ads for an advertising agency?

Nope....

Instead, they would be in business for themselves.

Don't fall for it!

We'll talk later how to cheaply start tracking all your sources of advertising, so you can know once and for all what is working and more importantly what isn't working, so you can stop flushing your hard-earned money down the toilet.

I personally wasted thousands of dollars before I decided to stop the madness.

You need to be able to account for every dollar you spend and tracking your sources will help you do just that.

Why in the world would you keep spending money on marketing that isn't working?

When business starts to slow down, the first thing most appliance repair companies do is cut back on their advertising which in most cases is a HUGE mistake.

Now think about this...

When your competition decides to cut back, then it becomes the best time to ramp up your advertising.

Why? you may ask

Because regardless of the economy, there are going to be consumers that need to find an appliance repair company when their appliances break down.

The key is using highly targeted Marketing that will only attract prospects you know you can help. More importantly, these types of advertising sources will allow you to track where your customers are coming from.

Then you will be able to CUT the FAT from your advertising budget by eliminating the sources that are not working and instead put more money into the strategies that you know for a fact are working.

Doesn't that make a whole lot more sense?

You may also be wondering, what those highly targeted sources of advertising are? Its online marketing sources, now not all are effective, but we will discuss the ones you should be focusing on throughout his book.

Chapter 4 - Your Ideal Customer Is Online, Are You?

This is exactly why most appliance repair businesses are getting online! They are using their websites to:

- Build trust, confidence and the start of a stable relationship with new and existing customers by providing educational tips and special offers.
- Expand their service offerings and service area.
- Gain a competitive advantage over their local competition.

As an owner of an appliance service business, do you can't afford to miss such an opportunity?

If you don't have an online presence and your competitors do, then they have a competitive advantage, more and more of your competition will soon figure it out and implement the strategies outlined in this book. Since your prospects and customers are already online, it won't be long before you lose them to a competitor if your company isn't online. Never before has there been such an inexpensive way to advertise your appliance repair company and skyrocket your return on investment.

The Internet does just that!

Let's shift gears now and talk about some of my favorite sources of online marketing, there are tons of options, but I don't want to overwhelm you, so instead, we will focus on the ones that can generate new customers for you in a short period of time.

Here they are:

- Google Maps
- Google AdWords
- Yelp
- Craigslist

- Lead Generation Providers.

In the next few chapters, we will discuss each of these sources in greater detail and show you how to get set up.

Chapter 5 - How to Get Your Appliance Repair Company Ranked On Page One Using Google Maps

Before I show you how to set up your appliance repair company on Google Maps, let me first tell you why it's on my list of recommended sources of finding new customers:

- **It's Free!** – Even if you don't have a website, which you should, you can get a free Google Map listing that will help with establishing your online presence.
- **Google is the largest search engine that means** the majority of your ideal customers are using it, there are several ways you can get on Google, such as SEO (Search Engine Optimization) takes a while to get on the first page, and it is the most expensive Options. Google AdWords will get you on the 1st page almost instantly, but if you don't know what you are doing it can get really expensive, very fast.
- Google Maps, on the other hand, is free, it can be set up in less than an hour, and if you are in small to medium size town, you can be on the 1st page of Google for free.

If you were to search on Google for any local business near you, you would notice that there is a section on the search engine that will show 3 Google Map listings. If you claim your Google My Business listing for your appliance repair company and get those listing to rank at the top of Google Maps, this will significantly increase the number of local consumers to find your business when they are looking for an appliance service company. In this article, we discuss the 3 most important factors that you need to do in order to get your appliance repair business ranked at the top of Google Maps.

32% Of Consumers Searching On Google For An Appliance Repair Company Click On The Google Map Listings

What we're going to cover includes:

The latest updates with Google Maps listings

The 5 biggest issues that could be preventing you from ranking in the Google Maps

Our proven model for ranking in the new 3 pack of the Google maps

And we're going to discuss some tools that you can use to systematize and automate the heavy lifting when it comes to managing and optimizing your Google Maps.

Why Is Google Maps Important For Appliance Service Companies That Want More Appliance Job Leads?

The image below is from a study done by Bright Local earlier in 2018, that shows which sections of the Google Search Engine Results Page gets the most clicks from consumers.

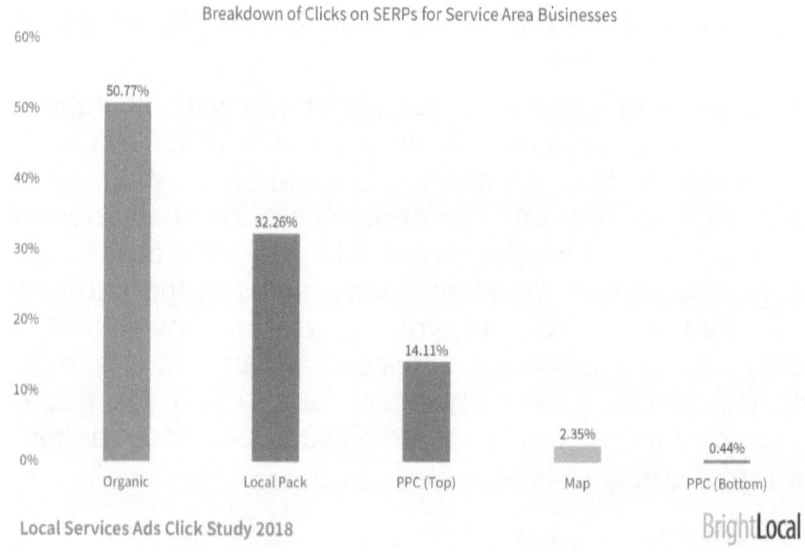

As you can see, the organic results are somewhere about 50 percent of the traffic or the consumers that search for a local business are clicking. You may have heard rumors that SEO is dead, or Search Engine Optimization is not working anymore.

SEO is how you can get your appliance repair business to show up in the organic results which currently is getting the majority of clicks from consumers.

The next most popular section to get leads from would be the local pack or the local map pack that's delivering 32 percent of clicks.

And then the pay per click ads at the top of the search engine results page, that's at 14%.

The map results are just above 2%. Now, the map results that we're talking about here is not the local 3 pack, but instead, it is if a consumer goes directly to Google's Map page.

The PPC ads at the bottom is less than 1%.

Google maps is important because it's the second biggest driver of appliance repair job leads for appliance service companies.
The Biggest Changes With Google Maps

The Google Local Pack used to display 7 appliance repair companies, now only 3 companies are being displayed. Google is basically making more room for ads since that is where they make majority of their money.

Now, just to give you a visual of how the search engine results page has changed over the years.

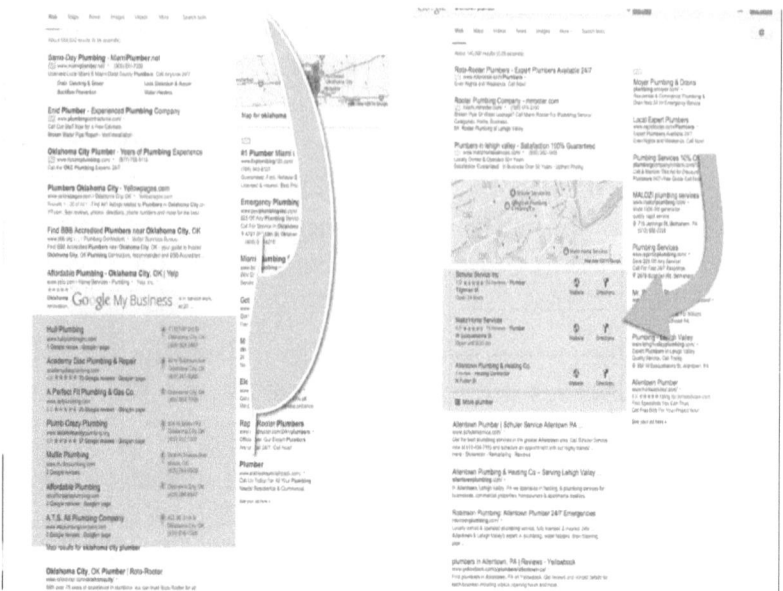

On the left side of the image is what it used to look like, where they had the ads at the top and along the right side, then you have the organic results, and in that area highlighted in green, used to be the 7 pack.

The image on the right is more similar to what it looks like today, where you have the ads at the top and then the maps. So, there are no longer the organic results in between the ads and the map section.

As you can see the map listings have been reduced from 7 to 3 listings, which is most commonly known today in the online marketing space as the 3 pack. There's a big opportunity for you if you're one of those appliance repair companies that show up in the 3 pack.

If you were in the original 7 pack, then once Google reduced the listings to 3, you probably have seen a reduction in your leads.

Google has also started showing ads in the map results, so not just only on the regular Google search engine results page, and now they're also testing home service ads in major metropolitan areas like Atlanta, Dallas and multiple cities within California.

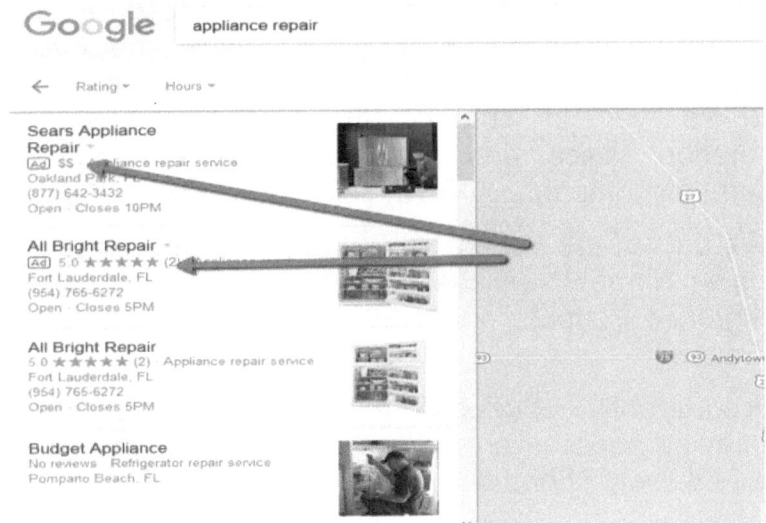

If you wanted to join their new home services program, you would have to go through a verification process, which is very similar to the HomeAdvisor type of setup.

Google's Home Service Ads show at the very top, then the regular ads and then the google maps.

The home service ads are set up as a lead generation type of format, where you don't pay each time someone clicks on the Ad, but instead, you pay per call. This is Google's way of entering the appliance repair lead generation space and competing with big-name lead generation companies like Angie's List and HomeAdvisor.

As part of the verification process to participate in the Google Home Services. They are going to do a background check, provide proof of licenses and insurance.

It's currently not offered nationwide yet, but so far, they are having success so if it's not provided in your service area however, it should be soon.

Home Service Ad creates more of an opportunity for you to dominate the first page results on Google.

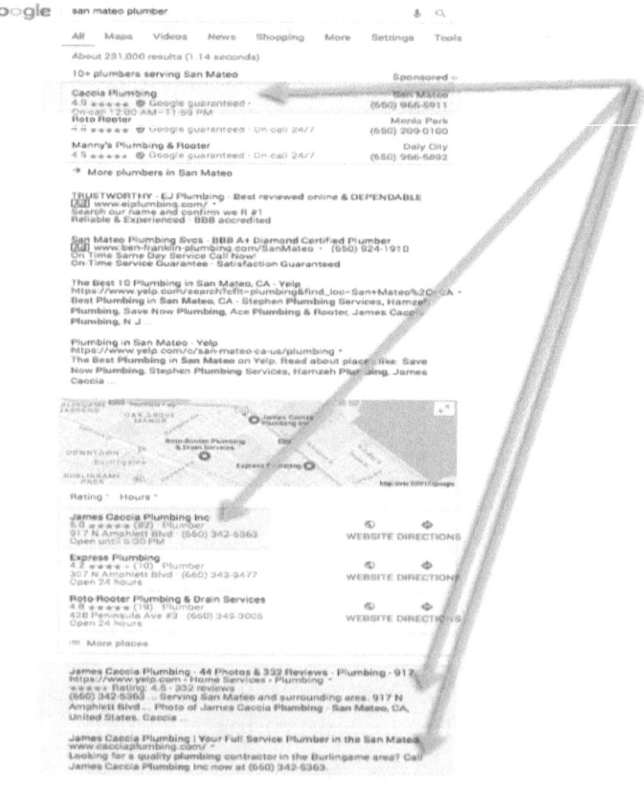

Now there are 4 sections on the search engine results page that you can have your appliance repair company displayed:

Google Local Service Ads Section
The regular Google Ads or Pay Per Click Section
The Google Maps listings
And then there are the Organic Search results

Now when you get into the organic search results, there is even more opportunity, because you could even have multiple listings there along with your appliance repair website. You could have your yelp listing showing up there, and any other directory site such as Yellow Pages and Angie's List.

These changes by Google provide more opportunity for appliance service businesses to dominate their local service area.

Can't Seem To Get Your Google Map Listing To Rank Higher?

Let's talk about what could be hurting your google maps rankings. Maybe you already claimed your Google maps listing, but for some reason, you just can't get it to show up in the top 3 results for the Google maps listings.

The first problem we will discuss is that you may have an inconsistent name, address, and phone number profile across the different citation websites.

And when you hear me reference citations, what I'm talking about are basically directory websites, such as Yellow Pages, Angie's List and Yelp. These are all examples of what citations are, and there are hundreds of them that you can get your local appliance repair company listed on.

Your appliance repair company may already be listed on a few hundred citations that you are not even aware of because some of these citations or directory websites use software to collect information on the web. So, without your knowledge or permission, there may already be a listing of your company on these sites.

If you have inconsistencies with your name, address, phone number, profiles, which could be caused if you've ever changed any of these things over the years, they could be hurting your map ranking.

The next thing is that Google has started to crack down on companies that use their main keyword as their company name instead of their real business name.

Let's say your real company name is John's Appliance, but you used Appliance Repair San Diego as your company name because that was a strategy a few years ago, to get into the top rankings on Google maps.

They're starting to crack down on listings like these that have keywords as company names. If you have that type of situation, you may want to consider changing it to your registered company business name.

The next thing is that you want to see if you have enough reviews across the web. Reviews alone won't help you to rank at the top unless you are in a very low competition area.

It's not uncommon for appliance repair companies that have a lower number of reviews to rank higher than their competition that may have 10 times the amount of reviews.

Reviews are important, but they are just one piece of the Google Map ranking puzzle.

If you find yourself in this situation where you have more reviews than your competition and even better reviews that them, then you may want to look into getting more citations.

Citations and Reviews are the main things I want you to focus on if you want to rank in the local map results.

There are multiple things that you can do to rank in the Google Maps, but we like to simplify things. And if you ever heard of the 80 / 20 principle, then you know that 20 percent of your efforts give you 80 percent of the results.

Below are the 20 percent of ranking factors that you should focus on:

The first thing you want to do is go ahead and claim your Google Map listing if you haven't already, then start getting citations. I'm going to give you some resources shortly to help automate getting your appliance repair business listed on these citation websites. If you're a one-person operation, and you have more time on your hands, then you can get these citations yourself and save some money.

It's nothing hard to do, but it can be time-consuming because there are a lot of directory sites. Essentially all you have to do is create an account on each of these directory sites and input your company's name, phone number, address, short description and your website.

The next important factor to focus on is reviews

If you've ever watched any of our training videos or read any of our other blog posts in the past, you always hear us stress that reviews are going to become more and more important as we go forward.

Consumers are starting to look at reviews first before calling an appliance repair company. So, you want to have reviews. You don't necessarily have to have the most reviews to rank in that top 3 position, but you want to have some reviews because it helps consumers to make the decision to call your appliance repair company instead of your competition.

The next thing is the on-page SEO for your appliance service website. Google is looking for an optimized appliance repair website that's linked to your Google Map listing.

Now that doesn't mean you have to go out now and create a website if you don't have one, because Google maps also give you a free website. What you want to do is make sure that you have the name, address, and phone number listed on your website. Most companies will list that on the bottom of the website. If you choose the option of going with the Google maps website, you want to just list that somewhere in the about us section of the website, and then that will take care of that optimization step.

Quick Checklist:

Make sure you have the login for your Google My Business account.

Make sure your company name is your registered company name.

Add your website address – This is getting a link from Google, which is probably one of the most authoritative links you could ever get. So, by claiming your listing and doing some basic set up, you can get this important link, and that's going to help you rank in the search engines, not just maps, but also in the organic search results.

Then you want to **use a local phone number**, don't use an 800 number for several reasons. Google is looking for that local number as well as consumers are looking for that local number. Most consumers don't want to deal with a large nationwide company. They're looking for that local company that's close to them. 800 numbers normally communicates to them that it's a big company and consumers will think that they have to pay more, or they may have to wait longer to get an appliance repair technician out to their home to fix their appliances. Consumers prefer just to call a local appliance repair company that's close by and who won't overcharge them for appliance repairs.

Add a local address. You can hide it if you are using your home address, but you still need to list it, so that Google knows where to show your listing.

Upload Photos – as many as possible; pictures of the owner, technicians and all the staff members are also good ideas. You can also upload pictures of your office if you have one, tools or equipment, and your service vehicles. People connect and resonate with people. And you can leverage this to update your google map list and to make it better converting.

List your hours of operation

List the different appliance repair services that you offer. More is better when it comes to optimizing your google map listings.

List multiple categories – Google My Business currently offers these categories for appliance repair companies: appliance repair service, refrigerator repair service, washer, and dryer repair service, and microwave oven repair service. Add all these categories if you service all those appliances because multiple categories will help your listing to rank for more searches which equals more appliance repair leads.

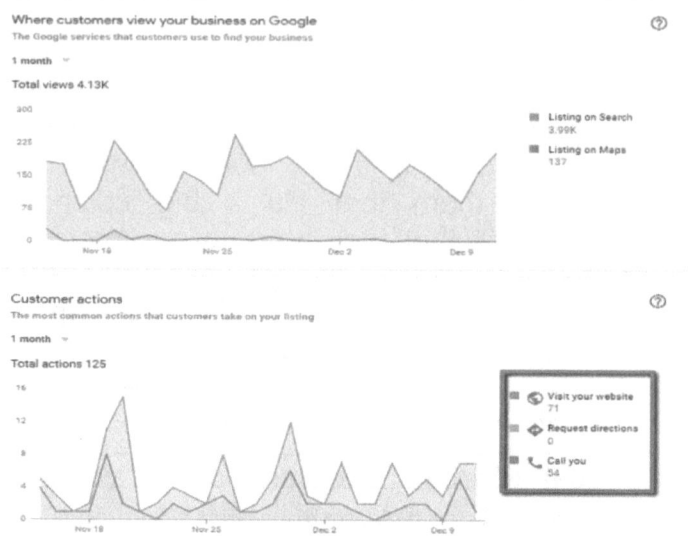

Above is a screenshot of inside a google map listing. So, this is why it's important to claim and get your login details, so you'll have access to this information.

This is in the insights section of the Google My Business listing and Google provides you with a lot more information than what you see in the image. That includes new keywords that you may want to target. The appliance repair keywords shown are actual keywords that people or consumers type in to find your listing.

And if you're doing any type of Search Engine Optimization or Pay Per Click Advertising, you can use those keywords to help you rank for additional keywords from those sources.

In the red box, you will see that 71 visitors came to this website, and the listing generated 54 calls.

Last year it used to be that if you could get your listing to rank in the 3 pack, for the main city within a county, then your listing would show up in the 3 pack for all the cities within that county, however things have changed this year with Google moving to a Mobile First Index.

With map listings now and mobile devices being the main search tool for consumers, Google uses the GPS coordinates from a consumer's phone to deliver a list of appliance repair companies in the map results that are closest to the consumer.

So, this is another reason that if you were getting a lot of appliance repair leads from google maps in the past and you've seen that leads have been reduced earlier this year, it's all about proximity now. Google is delivering the appliance repair company results that are closest to the consumer. While some appliance repair company may have seen less leads from Google Maps, there are others that are starting to see leads that they haven't seen before. Because of the proximity factor, their listings are now being shown more than they were shown before the Mobile First Index was introduced.

Create Citation Listings With Consistency

You want to have the exact name, address, phone number, and use the exact format and spelling. For example, if you spell out the word Street for one citation, then best practice is to continue to spell out the word street for all citations, don't get lazy and use ST as the abbreviation for street on some, because this will affect your rankings, or should I say lack of results in your ranking.

Your Google Map listing rankings are sensitive to things like these, so it's important to pick one format or spelling and do it for all your citations.

It's good practice to do a check to see how your company information is listed on all these different citation sources online. This way you can check for old or inaccurate data or in some cases you may even find duplicate listings, which you should either delete or if you find incorrect information you want to go ahead and update.

Pay Attention To The Big Data Aggregators

There are 4 big data aggregators: Factual, Axiom, Infogroup and Neustar. These companies distribute your business information to over 300 online directory sites. Now, let's say you changed your business address and updated your yelp and yellow page listings. That doesn't mean that these aggregators were updated as well. So, if you have inconsistencies, you want to actually go to these aggregator websites and also update your company information there, so that the aggregators can update all the websites that they provide information to.

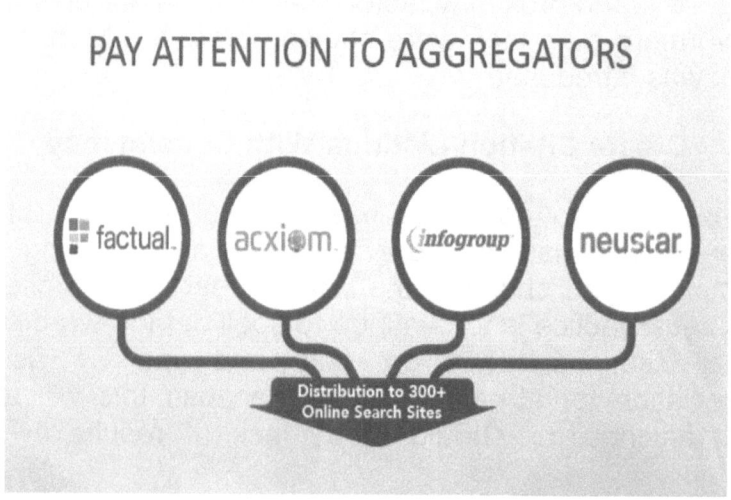

If you know that you are lacking some citations and you want to get started, getting some or adding additional ones, I wanted to provide you with some tools, so you can either do it manually or you can hire someone to do it.

Best Tools for Citations

Here are some resources to help you get the job done:
Bright Local – www.brightlocal.com
White Spark - www.whitespark.ca
Advice Local – www.advicelocal.com
Moz Local – www.moz.com/products/local
Yext– www.yext.com

All these companies offer different packages to help you get more citations and update any inconsistencies, outdated or incorrect information about your business.

Top Citations For The Service Industry.

Citation Site	D.A.	Country	Free / Paid	Listing URL
networx.com	50	USA	Paid	Click here
contractors.com	39	USA / CAN	Paid	Click here
Fixr.com	49	USA	Free	Click here
buildzoom.com	46	USA	Paid	Click here
bestplumbers.com	50	USA	Free	Click here
homeblue.com	42	USA	Paid	Click here
plumbingweb.com	39	UK	Free	Click here
reliableremodeler.com	33	USA	Free	Click here
directory.myhammer.co.uk	32	UK	Free	Click here
tradwebdirectory.com	26	USA	Free	Click here
ehardhat.com	27	USA	Free	Click here
theconstructioncentre.co.uk	35	UK	Free	Click here

The main ones that would apply to appliance repair companies are:

Contractors.com
Fixr.com
HomeBlue.com

These are smaller citations when compared to Yellow Pages or Yelp, but these are focused more on the service industry. Unlike the larger citations, they bring something else to the table. Since these are more relevant to the appliance repair industry, these will provide an extra push to improve your website and Google Map rankings.

If you want a list of some of the bigger citation sources, you can check out this page on how to establish a consistent NAP for your appliance repair Google My Business Listing.

Get Customer Reviews And Lots Of Them!

If you are not already getting reviews on a daily basis, I highly recommend that you start doing this. Your techs or other staff members should be asking for reviews after every service call.

Implementing a strategy to get consistent reviews, will not just help with Google Maps, but they will also help with any type of online marketing. Good customer reviews send a signal to Google and consumers that you are a trusted company.

I know getting reviews can sometimes be a tedious task and as an appliance repair business owner or manager, you already have a lot on your plate, from making sure every single phone call is answered to ordering parts.

The good news is that you can leverage certain tools to automate the request for a review after every single service call

Consider getting printed review cards that your technicians could actually leave with the customer once they complete the repair.

Train your techs to plant the seed and deliver a world class experience on every single service call so that the customer actually wants to leave a review, without the technician even asking.

Have a staff member call each customer a few days after the service call is done, just to follow up with the customer that everything is working fine. Very few appliance repair companies do this, and it's a great way to stand out from your competitors, get a good review and to earn more referrals.

Build the collection of reviews into your company culture

Getting reviews should be part of your normal daily process, just like how it's normal for the person answering the phone at your appliance repair company to tell the customer what service call fee is.

If you're a bigger operation and you want some tools to help automate the process, here are a few that you can use. The reason I'm giving you all these tools, instead of just recommending that you do it manually, is because if you can introduce automation in your business, then things will get done, 100% of the time.

Usually, if you have to leave it up to a person, they can be busier on some days that others and before you know it, 2 months went by and you have not gotten any new customer reviews.

Introducing software into your business will make sure that things get done every single day. Below are some services that will help to automate your review process:

Best Tools for Review Automation

Review Buzz – www.reviewbuzz.com
Birdeye– www.birdeye.com
Customer Lobby – www.customerlobby.com
Service Titan - www.servicetitan.com

These are listed in any specific order as far as quality is concerned, so we just wanted to make sure that we gave you several options to choose from. Some you may have already heard of as they may have already solicited you in the past. Any of these review services are great ways to make review automation a regular part of your business and that will do a lot of the heavy lifting for you because these services will do things like automatically sending an email to the customer or a text requesting the review once a service call is completed, all happening with very little human intervention, once everything is set up.

Service Titan is for larger appliance repair operations that helps with managing service calls, and it now integrates with these review automation companies. So once Service Titan is updated with the service call, it will automatically trigger this other software to go ahead and start the review collection process.

Action Items:
- Manually claim and optimize your Google My Business listing.
- Fill out as much information as possible, try not to leave any section blank.
- Upload plenty of pictures.
- If you have a promotional video for your company, you can upload that to your listing as well.
- Get listed in all the major data aggregators
- Leverage tools like Bright Local and White Spark.
- Make collecting reviews from existing customers a daily practice.

Chapter 6 - Increase Your Appliance Repair Leads With Paid Search

Pay Per Click Advertising is one of the best sources for appliance repair businesses that are looking for fast scalability and increase appliance service leads. With PPC marketing you can have your finger on the switch to turn on and off leads on-demand to increase phone calls into your appliance repair company.

In this chapter, we show you how to increase your appliance repair leads and how to maximize your Return On Investment using paid search, even if you or your previous account manager failed with Paid Pay Per Click Marketing in the past.

Overview Of What You Will Learn:

- **Keys To Success With AdWords** – You have to understand some key elements with Google AdWords if you want to succeed with Pay Per Click Advertising.
- **Why Quality Score is important and how to maximize it** – the quality score of your ads can lower the cost per click and as a result lower your cost per lead
- **How to structure your campaign and adgroups for success** – Having multiple Ad Groups, segmenting your keywords, writing compelling text ads, use of site extensions to get an advantage and creating high converting landing pages are critical if you want to win with PPC Ads.
- **Why KPI's (Key Performance Indicators) Are Your Best Friends** – Don't spend another penny on paid search without putting the proper tracking in place so you can determine what's working and more importantly what's NOT working...

So why PPC should be part of your Internet marketing…

You want leads quickly; you don't want to wait for days, weeks or months to get your phone ringing with appliance service requests, which is what happens when you're doing things like SEO.

In some cases, Search Engine Optimization can take 8-12 months to start seeing anything consistent as far as leads are concerned, but with Pay Per Click Marketing, you can pretty much set up an Ad and have leads the same day, that's one of the main benefits of using PPC.

Your AD can show up as often as possible when consumers are looking for appliance repair. If you want to have a 24-hour campaign to capture as much leads as possible, you could potentially do that.

But if you are like most appliance repair companies that only operate on a 9am – 5pm schedule, you can set up your campaigns to only run during those hours. But if you want to also set up an after hour schedule and charge a little bit extra for emergency service, if that's something you offer, you can do that with PPC advertising as well.

Get your ads to show for none geographically related search terms. What I mean by that, is a keyword without the city attached to it.

So, assuming you're in San Diego, one of the most common search terms is going to be appliance repair, San Diego.

But not all consumers are going to type the city name along with the keywords.

Consumers are getting lazier, and they want to do the least amount of work as possible. So instead of typing the city name, now they're just doing appliance repair.

Or if it's a refrigerator problem, they may just do fridge repair.

In either scenario, you want your ads to show up for both variations of the search term, PPC marketing allows you to show up for either version of a particular keyword.

Want unlimited scalability?

If you wanted to take over your local market, and you can afford to spend a large budget on advertising with PPC, you could pump a lot of money into your campaigns.

However, with something like SEO, even if you had $10,000 a month to put into a campaign, there's only so much an SEO company can do for you.

And the reason is it's not all up to the SEO company, right?

There are certain factors that are out of their hands, and what I'm referring to here is Google.

An SEO company can't control what Google will do.

They know a few things that Google likes, but they don't know everything that Google likes. So, they can only move at a certain pace, and if they do things too fast, then there is a risk that your appliance repair website will get penalized and will not rank in the search engines.

With Pay Per Click advertising if you want to scale fast and spend $10,000 today, you could and there would be no penalties from Google AdWords.

Next, let's talk about why appliance repair PPC campaigns fail.

Now, this is really important because most appliance repair company owners that try paid search advertising, end up thinking it's a waste of time or they lost so much money doing it.

Learning to run a successful Pay Per Click campaign, requires its own set of unique skills, just like with appliance repair. That is its own skillset.

While a handyman may be used to fixing things around the home, he may not be best person to fix an appliance.

Most online marketing companies that offer Pay Per Click management services don't offer Search Engine Optimization because they are two different services that require different expertise.

The #1 reason though is that most appliance repair companies failed to understand the way the AdWords auction process works and the complexity of the industry.

Google AdWords promotes paid search as an easy thing to do and they even offer free account managers. But if you have ever tried PPC advertising in the past and you couldn't get it to work for your appliance business, then you know it's far from easy.

This is what it looks like when most appliance repair business owners set up an AdWords Campaign.

They put up an ad with 10 to 20 keywords, and they let the campaign run.

They set up one ad group for all the different appliance repair services they offer such as:

Refrigerator repair, Dryer repair, etc.

All their keywords go into one ad group when it should be separated at a minimum by the different service types.

Refrigerator repair should have its own ad group; stove repair should have its own ad group and so on and so forth.

They don't use specific text ads and landing pages for each ad groups or keywords.

What I mean by that is most appliance repair companies create one generic ad.

"We provide appliance repair in your local service area. We've been in business xyz years"

If you're targeting refrigerator repair leads, that ad should be something about refrigerator repair and **NOT** just appliance repair.

If a consumer is searching for something like "my refrigerator is not cooling," that exact phrase should be in your Ad or other variations of it like:

Is your refrigerator broken?

Is your fridge not cooling?

Those things will get consumers to click on your ad because it's specific to what you're looking for.

If you are sending consumers to the home page of your appliance repair website after they click on your AD, you are losing serious money!

Instead of the home page of your site, you should be sending consumers to a specific page on your site that is related to what they are search for. This is what is known as a landing page of your website.

If the consumer has a refrigerator problem, you want them to go to the refrigerator repair page on your website.

If you are doing any form of paid search advertising and your website doesn't have a page for all the different appliance repair services you offer, then you'll want to get that page A.S.A.P because until you do, you will continue to lose money with PPC marketing.

Speaking of landing pages let's talk about how to make those better converting.

Make sure to have a strong call to action or offer on the landing page. Now this applies to both the ad and the landing page.

If you are not familiar with the term "Call To Action" what I mean by a call to action is that you want to tell consumers what you want them to do and with the case of appliance repair, the #1 action you want them to take is to **Call Now!**

Another example of a call to action is for the consumer to visit your website. But I'm a big believer in getting them on the phone!

Because sometimes consumers that go from the ad to the website, they get distracted somewhere in between that and never end up calling. And in the case with PPC advertising you just paid for the consumer to click on your ad even though they didn't end up calling your appliance service business.

Now let's talk about how to structure and set up your pay per click marketing campaign for minimum costs per lead and maximum return on investment.

The first thing I want to recommend that you have in place is **conversion tracking**.

Now this is very important because this is going to tell you if PPC advertising is working for you or NOT, you really should have conversion tracking on any form of advertising you're doing, whether it's online or offline, but we'll just stick to the subject of PPC from now.

PPC conversion tracking is going to tell you things like:

How many clicks is it taking you to get a phone call? Why is that important? Because that's going to start to tell you how much it costs you to acquire a lead.

A lead for an appliance repair company is a person that actually calls with a need for major appliance repair, right?

So, you want to be able to track things like that, to see the effectiveness of your campaign.

Leverage FREE ad extensions to make your ad stand out on the page.

Ad Extensions make your Ad bigger but at no additional cost. Unlike traditional advertising like with a magazine or newspaper who charge you the bigger size ad you want.

If you have ever advertised with your local newspaper, then you know they offer different size ads, there is the full-page ad, 1/2-page ad, classified ad, etc.,

If you do your Pay Per Click AD extensions correctly, it will be like a half page ad versus a regular ad without the extension, which is more like a classified ad.

It doesn't cost anything extra for you to have ad extensions, so you definitely want to use it to your advantage, and you will be rewarded with more clicks, which is ultimately going to lead to more phone calls.

Never Stop Testing Your Ads

You want to do ongoing AD split testing so that you can tweak and fine-tune your Ad performance over time. PPC advertising is not one of those, set it and forget it advertising mediums. It's something that you must optimize on a daily or at a minimum on a weekly basis.

Once you find an ad that works, you should try and test to see if you can find an even better ad to improve the performance of your campaign.

A better ad that converts better will improve the quality score of your ad, which as a result, brings down the costs of your clicks.

As an appliance repair business owner, you're always trying to see if you can lower costs and maximize your return on investment. Split tests is one way you can do that.

Don't even think about spending another penny until you have conversion tracking in place.

Now let's talk about some conversion tracking. Essentially, you should have a dynamic phone number that swaps from PPC, organic or direct traffic. What that will do for you, is tell you exactly where your appliance service leads are coming from.

Are your leads coming from Google AdWords?

Did they come from your SEO efforts?

Or was it a referral from an existing customer that already knew what your website address was?

It's important not just to know that you received 300 leads this month, but you also want to know what source of advertising those leads came from.

You need to know so you can better optimize how you spend your money.

Maybe you'll find out that one source of leads is not working as well, so you can maybe minimize the budget there.

You don't necessarily have to turn it off because you may still be getting leads from it. But if you realize that PPC is working a lot better for you than Yellow Page Ads, then this information will tell you to spend more money with PPC marketing.

Dynamic phone numbers help separate the different sources of leads, and it also helps you track phone calls back to the keyword and the campaign that provided the lead.

This is important because you may end up with hundreds if not thousands of keywords in paid search campaign and it's important to know which keyword is working the best.

This will allow you to focus more on the ones that work and for the ones that are not working you can consider eliminating from your campaign.

And then your campaign will just be left with actual keywords that generate leads for you regularly.

Deleting non-performing keywords will improve the overall quality score of your campaign, which will result in lower costs per click.

Then there's web form tracking.

If you have a contact form on your website for consumers to fill out, which you should, because not all consumers are going to be able to call you, especially during normal business hours, some consumers can't be on the phone while they're at work.

Having a web form on your website is a great way to capture, some additional appliance repair leads for those people that can't necessarily speak on the phone during normal business hours.

Important key performance indicators or K.P. I's, when it comes to PPC.

Total Ad spend – how much you spend in each month

Average cost per click

How many clicks does it take you to get a phone call?

Average cost per lead – you need to know this for calls as well as web forms.

If you're running an efficient campaign, what you can expect to see with Pay Per Click advertising is somewhere in this range of $5 – $40 per lead.

You want to be able to track your return on investment.

Is this PPC thing really working for us?

This can vary from city to city, country to country. So, you want to be able to track this data, so you can know what's really working for you.

Keyword MATCH types matter.

There are different keyword match types:

- **Exact Match**
- **Phrase Match**
- **Broad Match**
- **Broad Match Modifier**

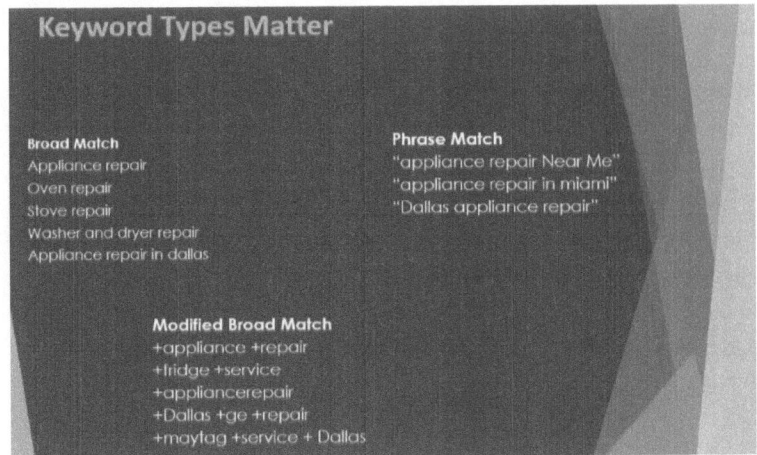

The first one we're going to take a look at here is the **Broad Match.**

Think about these as the most expensive keywords for you. The reason is these are the ones that are going to bring in unrelated searches.

The keyword Appliance Repair as a Broad match means Google could pretty much send you any type of consumer, as long as it has to do with repair. So, if someone was looking for a car repair, lawnmower repair, etc., your broad match keyword and Ad could show up for these types of searches. So, you want to monitor those very closely.

That's the downside of the broad match, but also broad match is going to bring you good keyword searches as well.

To help minimize what your Ads will show for, you should monitor your negative keywords, which we're going to talk about a little bit later.

Next is the **Phrase Match** Type, and this match type has quotes around the keyword. You could still get some negative searches from it, but not as much when compared to the Broad Match type. Phrase match means that the words must be contained in the keyword and in the exact order.

Modified Broad Match

Now, this is similar to the phrase match type, but you can have words before it or after it. What I mean by that, is the search term must have the word appliance repair, but it can also include other words before or after the words "appliance repair." For example, same day appliance repair or appliance repair near me.

Negative Keywords Can Make Or Break Your Campaigns

Here are some negative keywords that you want to look out for:

- Jobs
- Parts
- Warranty
- Blender
- Mixer

And a matter of fact, if you don't have these in your campaign, you should add them right after you finish reading this chapter.

Some of the common negative searches that we see show up have to do with jobs. You don't want to get people clicking on your ads looking for an appliance repair job, right?

If a consumer is looking to get their blender fixed and you don't service them, you don't want your ad to show up for searches like these because all these bad searches cost money.

Pay attention to your negative keywords; I recommend you check them daily, but at least on a weekly basis at a minimum.

Write compelling appliance repair ads that resonate with what consumers typed in to the search engines to entice them to click on your ad versus your competition.

When it comes to writing compelling text ads, less is more!

You want to be concise, tell them exactly what you want them to do. If you give consumers too much information, you will only confuse them.

If you have a special offer, like $25 off service, you want to reference that in the ad. Including these things will help consumers to choose your appliance service company over your competition.

Here's an example of a company that's using the ad extensions.

```
Appliance Service in Austin | $65Off & Free Quote W/ Repairs
[Ad] www.repairmyapplianceaustin.com/ ▼  (512) 838-6447
Same Day Service @ North Austin - Round Rock - Cedar Park - Leander. Call Now! Professional
Technicians. Up to 1 Year Warranty. In-Home Appliance Repair. Neighborhoods: Austin, Lakeway,
Cedar Park, Round Rock, Leander, Pflugerville, Buda, Dripping Springs.
⦿ 3267 Bee Caves Rd, Austin, TX

    Refrigerator Repairs              In-Home Appliance Service
    Expert Refrigerator Technicians   Our Techs Carry 90% of the Parts
    We Repair All Makes & Models      Serving Austin & Surrounding Areas

Appliance Repair Austin Texas | 1 Year Warranty 20% Off Repair
[Ad] www.patriot-appliancerepair.com/AustinMetroArea/Fix_It_Today! ▼  (512) 903-0641
Prompt And Reliable Expert Technicians Appliance Repair Service ATX Metro Area. Fix The Problem
Today. Same Day Ser Call By 11AM. Services: Dryer Repair Service ATX, Refrigerator Repair.

20% Off Appliance Repairs | Sears®: #1 Appliance Solutions
[Ad] repair.searshomeservices.com/Appliance/Repair ▼
Wherever You Bought It, We'll Fix It. Schedule a Local Repair Expert Today!

First Class Appliances | Appliance Repair | firstclassaa.com
[Ad] www.firstclassaa.com/ ▼
Our Repair Technicians Are Fully Licensed And Insured. 20+ Years Of Experience
```

Look how big that first ad is compared to the other 3.

If we could match these up, the first ad is almost the size of all three ads combined.

Ad extensions makes the ad jump off the page.

Want To Get Your PPC Ads To Show Up In The Map Section Of The Search Results?

Ads in the Google Maps section is something relatively new. If you want your pay per click ads to show up here, you will need to enable the location ad extension.

Send consumers to a well thought out page on your website that's built to convert

Consumers that come across your appliance repair ads, typically have 2 options, either to call your appliance repair company from the ad or to click on the ad and visit your website. For the ones that click on your ad to find out more about what you have to offer, you will have to convince them with the information on that page, to call your appliance service company over the competition.

Have your phone number big and bold in the upper right-hand corner of your website. Now there are actually studies that show that when a consumer visits a website, where their eyes go first is that upper right-hand corner. This is why you want the phone number to be there.

When a consumer visits an appliance repair website, you don't want them spending a lot of time reading. Instead you want them to pick up the phone and call!

Appliance Repair is an emergency type industry...

If a consumer's fridge is broken and their food is spoiling, they just want an appliance repair technician to come out right now. So, while consumers may do some research before choosing an appliance repair company, it's very minimal compared to other industries. Most consumers just want to see a few good reviews, and that's enough for them to make a final decision.

Other conversion elements to consider adding to your website:

- **$25 off** – offering a discount to get the consumer to call.
- **Customer reviews** – if you don't have reviews on your site, you need to get them on there.
- **Answer questions that the typical consumer has in their mind** – honest expert service, no hassle upfront pricing, and 100% satisfaction guarantee.

Common questions in a consumer's mind when choosing an appliance repair company:

Am I going to get ripped off?

That's the main question a consumer has when they're calling any type of service company.

Does the appliance service technician have experience?

They want someone with experience that's going to fix the problem right then and there and not someone that just got out of appliance repair school.

Is my appliance worth fixing?

They don't want to dump a lot of money into an appliance that's not worth it, and if they do decide to get it fixed, they want to know the price upfront, so they can determine whether to get it repaired or just replace it.

What if there is an issue after the repair?

100% satisfaction guaranteed is telling them that, if there is a problem, the company is going to stand behind their service and do whatever it takes to make things right.

Now, one of the things that maybe going on in your mind is, PPC advertising seems complicated. I don't think I have time for it.

Afterall, you're running an appliance service business and taking care of all the day to day activities that comes along with that.

The truth is, you're going to make your most money fixing appliances, not trying to do the advertising yourself. However, if you're a small one-man operation, you are already wearing multiple hats.

You're the accountant, the marketing guy, the technician, and that's okay. But as soon as you get to the level where you can hire a company to do the advertising for you, then you should, to allow you more time to focus on the task that brings in the most money for your company, which is fixing appliances.

Now some of you reading this may have a larger operation, and you don't want to do the online marketing tasks yourself, and instead, you are considering outsourcing some of it, or maybe you want to hire an in-house person to start doing some of this for you.

Then your next question is how do I choose a good company to manage my PPC campaigns?

Here are a few questions that you'd want to ask them.

1. **How much of the budget that they're telling you to spend each month will go towards advertising versus their management fee.** How most PPC management companies work is they'll tell you how much you need to spend. For example, $5,000 per month and then they take a percentage of that, so the full $5000 doesn't go towards paying for ads. Others will add a percentage on top of the ad spend. Usually, that's somewhere between, I'd say 10 to 20 percent of what you spend. So, you're looking at about $500 to $1000 per month in management fees. If you hire a management company, you need to calculate their management fee into what is costing you per lead to see if it makes sense. A lot of people made this mistake, and they just use what they spend with Google AdWords as the only expense, but the management fees, is an additional expense, that must also be factored into your true cost per lead. Those extra management fees can be the determining factor of whether or not you have a successful campaign.

2. **What type of tracking will they put in place?** You want to be able to track a phone call versus someone that just entered their information into the web form. If you don't have web or call tracking that connects to AdWords, you'll be at a major

disadvantage with your competition. And you want to be able to, with the tracking to differentiate the different sources of your leads. Did the lead come from PPC or was it organic traffic? Tracking allows you to track your key performance indicators?

3. **Will they be setting up landing pages for you for each ad group?** – Ideally, you want to have separate landing pages instead of just to the homepage on the website. If they typed in dishwasher, you want to take them to a page on your website that is all about dishwasher repair. If they type in stove repair, it needs to go to a page on your website, all about stove repair.

4. **How will the pages be optimized for conversion?** They should be able to tell you what type of conversion elements are going to be on those landing pages. They should be able to show you examples as well.

5. **Are they going to split test the ads for each ad group?** And then how often will they conduct split test.

6. **Will they leverage ad extensions for you to make the Ad stand out in the search results?** And will they be tracking that to see whether the ad extensions work for your particular market?

7. **What are the targets in terms of cost per lead and return on investment?** They should have a goal for you.

ACTION ITEMS:

1. **Conversion tracking** – It's a must, without it, you could be losing a lot of money with PPC advertising.
2. **Use small Ad groups** – your campaign must be broken into smaller ad groups that target the different services that you provide.
3. **Create high converting Ads** – Your text ads must match what the consumer typed into the search engines. Now this isn't going to be always the case if you have an ad group with multiple keywords in there. Another option you can do, and this is somewhat advanced, is to have one keyword per ad group. And at that point, everything matches up at least 90 to 95 percent of the time.
4. **Understanding of keyword match types**– The broad match type is the one you must be very careful with. I usually recommend for someone just starting out with PPC advertising to starting out with exact match and phrase match and then work your way into the broad match modifier, if you're not getting any leads after a few weeks then consider testing broad match. But once you start running broad match, you want to check the negative keywords.
5. **Add negative keywords** – I highly recommend that if you're not checking those on a regular basis, that you start doing so on a daily or weekly basis.
6. **Write compelling text ads** – that resonates with what the consumer types in and entices them to click on your ad versus the competition. Remember they're seeing multiple ads, and what you use as your headline, is the main thing that is going to grab their attention. Then you have the description which helps to get more conversions.
7. **Consider using ad extensions**– to make your ads stand out more in the page. There're multiple extensions that you can use, to make your ad look bigger, and you'll get a lot more clicks with a bigger ad.
8. **Use Landing Pages with high converting elements** - Having the phone number, big and bold in the upper right-hand corner. Display your customer reviews, accredited by the better business bureau, if you are and lastly offer a discount.

Chapter 7 – The SEO Formula

The SEO landscape is forever evolving, and typically, when we're talking about SEO strategies, we're primarily focusing on the Google search engines versus Bing and Yahoo. That includes YouTube which is also considered to be a search engine. The reason is because Google does have about 80 percent of the market share. So primarily that's what we focus on as a company when we generate appliance repair leads for our clients using SEO.

Topics covered in this chapter:

- How to get your appliance repair website ranked in the search engines for your most profitable appliance repair keywords? Hint: You need to think beyond just appliance repair."
- How to increase the authority of your appliance service website so that your website pages will rank higher in the search engines.
- How to get relevant links for your website?
- Why duplicate content may be hurting your rankings?
- What are the most important online directories that you should list your appliance repair business in?
- Are bad links holding your website back, and how to get rid of them?
- What are the most important Appliance Repair Keywords that your website should be targeting?
- Which online review sites are the most important?

Does Search Engine Optimization still matter?

I get asked this question all the time. There are some gurus out there and some blogs that will say the SEO is dead and that it no longer works. Maybe you have experienced that, where you've tried it on your own, and you just don't seem to get any results.

Well, I'm here to tell you that we use it every day to generate hundreds of appliance repair leads to our existing clients. So, the quick answer is that YES it does matter.

3 biggest changes that we've seen with search engine optimization in the appliance repair industry:

1. You can no longer use duplicate content. Well, that's true to a certain extent.

It's not something that we recommend when we do consulting for appliance repair companies that are doing their own SEO. It still works, but we've seen sites that either doesn't rank well with it or they could even get a penalty because of the duplicate content.

If you ever heard of the Google Panda Update which they used to run once or twice a year, it's become part of the regular algorithm where it's actually done over 30 days.

So yes, you can still use duplicate content on your city pages, we use to use it probably 3 or 4 years ago where we just duplicated the content for each city page and just change the city name. But we've gotten away from it because we feel over the long-term Google will crack down on it, eventually.

We're starting to see an indication of poor ranking due to duplicate content if it's not done right, so we wanted to mention it. Since we don't think it fits into a long-term strategy, we recommend that you use original content.

2. If you have too many irrelevant or low-quality links pointing back to your site

This could be negatively affecting the rankings of your appliance repair website.

3. You need a real physical office address to rank in the Google Maps

In the past, some appliance repair companies used to use a virtual office address, or they use the U.P.S. store to get their appliance repair business listed in the Google Maps section of the search engine.

Google has pretty much cracked down on that, and you don't see too many appliance repair companies ranking in the maps section with those types of addresses, because of that.

You can still use your home address, and you don't have to display the address. That's definitely still working. But ideally, if you have an office that's definitely the way to go for that.

Most appliances repair companies serve a 10 to 25-mile radius. So, there are a lot of cities and a lot of towns, and to rank effectively across all those cities and all those towns, you need to have multiple individual city/town pages.

We usually get this question;

How do you rewrite the content for 20 to 30 different cities?

And that's what a lot of appliance companies, SEO agencies or even web design companies do; they would just use that duplicate content strategy. So, they only write the content once, and then they just copy it on to all the different city pages. So, if your appliance repair website is not ranking as you think it should, you may want to look into this.

If you want to check if duplicate content could be part of the problem why your appliance repair site is not ranking well, you can do an analysis check using a website called **Copyscape.com**. That site will work well to check duplicate content on one or a few pages because all you have to do is enter the domain name of your website and click on search. It's a paid service, but it's not expensive, and they charge based on the amount of words on the page. So, for a few dollars, you could quickly identify if your home page has a duplicate content issue.

Now if you have multiple pages on your appliance repair website, let's say you have 20 or 30 pages you may want to use another service, called **Siteliner.com**. This service will analyze all the pages on your website and let you know if there's any duplicate content across the web.

Ideally, you want to have unique content for each of those city pages, but it doesn't have to be 100 percent unique. You can probably get away with 70 or 80 percent uniqueness.

What if you do come across that your Appliance Service Website has duplicate content?

You don't have to delete it necessarily.

You can either choose to rewrite it, or you can add additional content, to help minimize the duplicated content.

If you want to test it, you can just try either rewriting or rewording the content on one of those pages and then track the results to see if the rankings change just by doing that.

Now if you do that, the next step is to get Google to visit that page so that they can update their index.

If you are not sure how to get Google to come to your site and do that, the easiest way is to sign up for **Google Webmasters** at https://www.google.com/webmasters/ if you don't already have one. It gives you a lot of insight in addition to having Google to crawl your site. Once you actually change the content and requested the crawl from Google, then give it a couple of weeks to see if the rankings change.

Google is taking a lot longer to crawl and update websites nowadays. So, two to four weeks ideally would be good to see if the rankings change.

Do you have too many low quality or irrelevant links pointing to your website.

A few years ago, it used to be all about links. The website that had the most links is the website that would get the number one position on Page 1 of Google.

Google cracked down on that.

Particularly the Penguin update addressed this, and it's now more about the **quality of those links** and the **relevance of those links** than it is the quantity. So, you may want to review your link profile for your website and find any bad links, and to either have them removed or disavowed.

You can get an idea of what your link profile looks like with your Google Webmasters Tools account, and this is also where you would want to disavow any bad links. You can identify these links to Google and tell them you don't want to have them associated with your website, which is what disavowing a link is.

They are not going to remove the links, but they're basically going to re-categorize them from a do follow link to a no follow link and then it won't negatively impact the rankings of your sites.

The disavow process is all you need to do, but if you also want to get them removed, you'd have to actually contact the website owner that is linking to your website and ask them to remove the link, which sometimes can be a challenge and Google knows this.

That's why they have the Disavow Tool, for website owners to discredit those links in the event of that type of situation. Now something to keep in mind, you can still get links even if you've never tried to get links.

That is just how the web works.

There are companies out there that are scraping information online and are always looking for different websites to link to. Let's say there's a new appliance repair directory. They will want to find every single appliance repair company in Houston. So, they're going to go to Google, and they're going to actually go through every single page and list every single appliance repair company that they can find and then they're going to take that information and add it to their appliance repair directory website. That's going to create a link back to your site. But that could be a low-quality link. While it may be relevant, it's a new directory.

Who knows what types of links are pointing to them?

It could be a low-quality link that you've received even though didn't ask them to link to you.

So, it's good to check your link profile as part of your monthly or quarterly strategy to take a look at the backlinks that are pointing to your Website and see if you notice any low-quality links. You can then disavow them or contact owners of those websites that are linking to you and ask them to remove the link.

As part of your monthly appliance repair SEO strategy, you continuously want to work to diversify the anchor text and build more high-quality and relevant links to your website.

Not sure what anchor text is? It's the text that is hyperlinked to your website.

The reason you want to have multiple anchor texts is because that's how you get your website to rank, for hundreds if not thousands of different appliance repair keywords.

Google Maps has a major change with the Google Penguin update, and it primarily addressed the local map listings.

It took a major toll on appliance service companies that were using fake addresses such as the U.P.S. store, mailbox, etc., They were the main ones that got affected. Google is trying to get more real physical business address in the map listings. But since the appliance repair industry is a service area business, and that's just a fancy way of saying appliance repair companies provide service at the customers' homes.

They understand that most appliance repair companies don't have an office for consumers to come to, they know that a lot of appliance service business owners operate from home and then they just have technicians that go out to the consumer's address.

That's why the home address is still working, and it probably will continue to work because they really do understand that appliance repair is a service area business.

If you're doing your own appliance repair search engine optimization and you're doing it the same way you used to do it four or five years ago, and you're not seeing the results, it's probably because of what used to work in the past is no longer working today. In the Panda, Penguin and Pigeon era, **it's all about the user experience now**, and there's something referred to as **user experience optimization**, which is now part of effective search engine optimization.

You typically hear of On Page SEO, Off Page SEO and now there's User Experience SEO.

The new appliance repair SEO formula requires a heavy focus on user experience. This is because Google is primarily focused on the end user. If the consumer goes to Google's search engines looking for an appliance repair company, they want to make sure they are delivering exactly what the consumer is searching for. So as a result, they track what the consumer is doing, and if they realize that the consumer is not finding what you're looking for, then they're going to change who ranks where on the first page of Google.

Search engines track everything! Literally!

So once someone goes to Google and they type in appliance repair to find a local service company, they track to see what the consumer does. That includes things such as:

- Do they scroll down on the search engine results page and which website do they click on?
- Then when they click on that website what do they do next?
- How long do they stay on that website?
- Are they watching a video on the website or are they clicking on links on the website?

These are all things that Google is tracking, including whether the consumer clicks the back button, which would indicate that they didn't find what they are looking for. Google is tracking all these things.

If that consumer now goes from Google to let's say Bing or Yahoo, they're paying very close attention to that because that's definitely not what they want to happen. So, click through rate is key when it comes to user experience optimization.

They're also looking at the scroll rate. Are consumers scrolling down once they get to your appliance repair website? Are they clicking on links? **The amount of time that they spend on your website is a big deal.**

This is where you want to track the bounce rate of your website, which is how long the consumer stays on your website before leaving. Do they come to your website and then leave? Do they leave in 10 seconds, 20 seconds? Ideally, you want each visitor to your website to be spending 3, 5, 10 minutes or more on your Website.

Now how do you track things like the bounce rate, time on site and click through rate?

You can track it with a free tool from Google, called **Google-Analytics.**

https://analytics.google.com/analytics/web/

I highly recommend that you sign up for a free account, so you can start looking at these factors. Because these factors can and will negatively affect the performance of your appliance repair website.

Another reason these factors are important is because **they can rank you on page 1 with less links**. If you can get this part right, you can use a lot less links to get onto the first page.

A good number of reviews, relevant links, and a good click-through rate score are pretty much the new ranking factors that you want to focus on. You want to figure out also what the most important appliance repair keywords are. That's based on your service area, and you also want to pay attention to the search volume.

Now how can you find out the most important keywords in your local service area.

Well, one of the free tools again is from Google, who does provide a lot of free tools that you can use to improve your online marketing. To get access to their keyword planner, you do need to set up a Google AdWords account.

https://ads.google.com/home/tools/keyword-planner/

You don't need to run ads, although if you do run ads with Google AdWords, you'll get access to a lot more details, but all you need to do is sign up for a free account to get access to the keyword planner. They may ask you for a credit card, but if you're not actually running ads, you'll never be charged for anything.

Identify all the appliance service keywords you want your website to rank for

Set up a great website with unique pages to target those appliance service keywords, that you found from doing your keyword research.

Now you know which appliance repair keywords are actually getting the most clicks.

Now you need to create pages with those keywords. So, you can start showing up in a search engine when someone types those keywords in your local service area. And you also want to have pages for each service.

For each city, you want to optimize your website for user experience. Then you want to optimize for SEO which includes on-site optimization. You also want to build authority by using offsite optimization and then next you want to track the results. So, you should be looking at your results monthly at a minimum. If you create new pages, you need to know where those pages are ranking in the search engines, because if the rankings increase that also results in more appliance repair leads.

So here are a few appliance repair keywords

appliance repair	135000 your city +	appliance repair
maytag washing machine	6600 your city +	maytag washing machine
appliance center	6600 your city +	appliance center
garbage disposal repair	6600 your city +	garbage disposal repair
lg repair	3600 your city +	lg repair
kitchenaid repair	2400 your city +	kitchenaid repair
ice machine repair	2400 your city +	ice machine repair
kenmore repair	1000 your city +	kenmore repair
kenmore appliance repair	1000 your city +	kenmore appliance repair
maytag repair near me	1000 your city +	maytag repair near me
refrigeration technician	880 your city +	refrigeration technician
refrigerator repair cost	720 your city +	refrigerator repair cost
dryer repair cost	720 your city +	dryer repair cost
dishwasher rack repair	720 your city +	dishwasher rack repair
best appliance repair	720 your city +	best appliance repair
bosch repairs	590 your city +	bosch repairs
reliable appliance repair	590 your city +	reliable appliance repair
electrolux repair	590 your city +	electrolux repair
appliance service near me	590 your city +	appliance service near me
frigidaire service	590 your city +	frigidaire service
appliance dealers	590 your city +	appliance dealers
gas oven repairs	480 your city +	gas oven repairs

There's definitely a lot more, and some of that will apply to you while others won't. You know for example if you don't service Bosch appliances, then you know those definitely won't matter to you. The second column represents search volume. You may be thinking some of those numbers are pretty large especially the first, but it's because it represents a nationwide average.

135,000 searches get done on a monthly basis for appliance repair across the U.S. You can get a list of the top 50 appliance repair keywords at our website.

https://www.appliancerepairmarketingsecrets.com/top-appliance-repair-keywords-seo/

Just to review, you want to have a strong website with good content, and that has a good user experience.

You want to also leverage multimedia to improve the on-page time. Having multimedia is one way to improve user experience.

But leveraging multimedia especially video will help keep the consumers on your website longer. That's because for them to take time to watch the video takes a few minutes, but you don't want a long video. Just having something for a couple of minutes is ideal.

What type of content should you make those videos about…?

You could have a video of the owner of the appliance repair company welcoming them to the Website talking about the different services and brands that your company specializes in.

You can even introduce your team members and the different technicians that will be coming out to their homes.

All those things will help you with user experience.

And then you want to have different pages for each of the different services. So, you could have one page for refrigerator repair, another one for dishwasher repair, another one for stove repair and so on.

Don't just list all the services on one page and you want to have multiple pages for each of the different cities that you service. So yes, you'll have one page for the main city but then there's all those different towns or suburb areas that you want to create pages for, because that's going to help you rank a lot easier than trying to get just one home page of your website to rank for 20 or 30 different surrounding towns or cities.

Again, we do recommend that you have unique content. You also want to have customer reviews on the City pages as well, as those will help with those pages not only ranking easier, but it will help with converting more visitors to those pages into actual customers.

Ideally, you want to get reviews that are on Google, Yelp or Yellow Pages and actually get it onto that particular city page where the appliance repair service was completed. All these things are great signals to Google to rank higher, as well as consumers who are looking for reviews nowadays before they actually pick up the phone to call.

Reviews are another way to improve user experience.

On-page Search Engine Optimization Tips

Unique content on every page.

The main keyword that you want to rank each page for should be both in the title and in the H1 tag.

The keyword that you want to target must include the city name, such as appliance repair + city or refrigerator repair + city.

For example, if you're in Dallas, you can have 'Dallas appliance repair' or 'Dallas dishwasher repair.'

A surrounding city that you may target around Dallas would be Garland Texas.

So 'Garland appliance repair' is what you want to have in your title and H1 tag for your Garland city page.

Then you have the Meta Description that really sells the click. Now, this is important once you get onto page one of Google as the Meta Description is where you want to put the Call To Action because consumers actually read it before deciding to click on your listing.

So why should the consumer click on your website vs. all the other websites and ads on the first page?

Is it because you have the best service in town?

Is it because you offer a free estimate if they go with the repair?

Those are just a few things you may want to consider putting into your Meta Description to convince the consumer to click on your website.

Now, this can be very effective, especially if you're not necessarily in a number one position on page one.

So, let's say you're on page one but you're in number two or number three position, then by optimizing the Meta Description of your website, you could get more consumers to click on your website versus just immediately clicking on the website that is in the number one position.

Then you should have your company name, address and phone number in the footer section of your website.

Consumers are looking for your contact information, and they want to see where your appliance repair business is located.

They want to see how close you are to their home. So that's why that's important.

And then you want to do blog posts or write articles on an ongoing basis to keep your site updated. The blog will help to not only keep your site updated, but blog posts that are optimized correctly can also help you to rank for additional keywords.

Examples of blog posts you can write about are:

Why isn't my refrigerator cooling and the possible causes?

Or why doesn't my oven heat up?

These are all great resources because consumers that are having these types of issues with their home appliances are not necessarily going to just type in "appliance repair" in the search engines, which is probably the most common search term that most appliance repair companies target, but instead some consumers are going to type in the problem they are having such as "refrigerator is not cooling" or "oven not getting hot". You want to rank for such keywords like these as well.

Let's talk about off page SEO

On page search engine optimization is important, but if you're on Page 5 – 10 of Google then how do you get to the first page?

This is where off page SEO comes in, to get your website closer to page one so that you can start to get visitors to your site. At that point, you can start optimizing for user experience.

Did you set up your Google My Business Listing?

You do that so that you can start ranking in the map results. Once that is done, the next step to improve your rankings is to start getting a lot of citations across the web. That's primarily from local directory sites like Yelp, Yellow Pages and your social media sites like Facebook.

Then you want to start asking for online reviews from all of your customers

You want to leverage tools. If you don't want to do it manually, then you want to leverage tools like Review Buzz, Customer Lobby and Birdseye. There are several tools that can help you with this, but you can do it manually.

Reviews are going to be even more important in the future. We are already seeing a pattern where **consumers want to read reviews before calling an appliance repair company**. This is why Yelp is as big as they are.

They're a multi-million dollar company now, and it's all based on consumer reviews.

They saw that pattern years ago, and they created a website based around consumer reviews, and now they are multi-million dollar company.

And I'm telling you reviews are going to become more and more important as time goes on, if you take away anything from this chapter, it's that you need to get on top of collecting customer reviews on a regular basis.

So, every single customer that you provide appliance repair services for, you should be asking them to leave a review. And it doesn't matter which review site they leave it on and they don't have to leave it on every single site.

Which Review Site Is Best?

Google is definitely my number one choice, and then Yelp would be the second choice. My third choice would be Facebook. Most of the other sites now pull reviews from those three, so those are the three you want to focus on.

But if you want to focus on one, it should be Google.

Now you're not going to please every single person, Right?

Someone's going to write a bad review of your appliance service company, and that's ok. That's just how it is. The important thing is that you get more good reviews than bad.

If you only had good reviews and no bad ones, then consumers would actually wonder how legitimate your reviews are.

You always want to **respond to all reviews whether good or bad**.

If you get a good review, you can just write a short note thanking the customer for choosing your appliance repair company and *let them know you understand they have a lot of choices when it comes to appliance repair, and you're happy that they chose your company and you look forward to serving them in the future.* That is an example of how you could respond to a good review.

When responding to a bad review, never blame the customer even if they are to be blamed. Instead, take responsibility for the bad outcome.

I always recommend to my clients to refund the customer their service call fee, if they think that will solve the problem. In most cases, it will. Not refunding the customer their money is not worth a bad review. Bad reviews are going to cost a lot more in new business in the future.

Get authority or relevant links to boost your rankings

What are authority links? Most directory sites especially the major ones are examples of authority links. Yelp is an authority link; Yellow Pages is also considered to be an authority link.

And then there are authority social media marketing sites like Facebook and Twitter.

Other examples would be:

- Better Business Bureau
- Angie's List
- Local appliance repair associations like the United Servicers Association and Professional Service Association.

If you could get a link from a manufacturer, let's say you are an authorized vendor for G.E. or Whirlpool and they link back to your website, those are also really good authority links, and they are extremely relevant.

A link from an appliance repair directory site is considered relevant. And then there are online article sites. If you publish an article about appliance repair and then link back to your website, it will be considered relevant.

A press release about your appliance repair company is considered both authority and relevant because the link will be from a newspaper or news station websites.

And if you publish monthly blog posts, other websites will pick them up and republish them. You'll get authority and relevant links back that way as well. Another way to find authority links would be to analyze your competition's websites on the first page of Google.

You'd need a software to do this, one of them that I would recommend is **majestic.com**, Majestic allows you to input your competitors that are ranking at the top of page one, and they will show you most of the links that your competitors have pointing to their appliance repair website. This software costs around $40 bucks per month, depending on the subscription you choose. Once you have the list of your competitors' backlinks, you can now contact the owners of those websites linking to your competition to see if you can also get the same links for your website.

As you analyze your competitors' websites and their backlinks, you need to understand something called Trust Flow.

Trust Flow (TF) is measured on a scale from 0 – 100, with "0" meaning the site has no Trust and "100" meaning it is the most trusted. So, the higher the TF, that will indicate if it's an authority link. Then you can just look in the domain name to see if it has anything to do with repair or appliance. That's how you could identify relevant links that your competition has, and then you can just contact the website owner to see how you can get a link from that website.

You don't have to reinvent the wheel

Learn from your competitors who are already on the first page of Google and replicate what they are already doing.

If you were to take a look at the top three sites on the first page of Google, there's a few things that you'll notice that they all have in common.

First, they all have in common a claimed and verified Google My Business listing.

Google used to have what's called a blended algorithm. So usually those three companies that will show in the top 3 map listings are also the same 3 websites that are at the top of the organic results. This, however, is not always the case anymore as the blended algorithm doesn't really work as it used to.

But if you do analyze the top 3 websites in the organic section to see if they have a Google map listing, in most cases, you will see that they have one. So that's why I would highly recommend that you set up your Google My Business (GMB) listing if you don't already have one.

Remember you can use your home address and you'll have the option not to display the address in the Google Maps. I highly recommend that you at least get this step going and you'll start to see some improvements in your organic results. And as well as you'll get more appliance repair leads just from being listed in the map results as some consumers go directly to maps section of the search engine to find an appliance repair company.

If you're setting up your GMB listing for the first time, use your real company name, don't try to get a keyword in there as that is considered spammy in Google's eyes. Example, don't do appliance repair Houston when your company name is dependable appliance.

While using a keyword instead of your real company name might still work to get you higher rankings, we don't recommend it as a long-term strategy. We're always thinking long term, and we want to get lots of online reviews, and as a reminder getting online reviews should be part of your daily routine.

Just like your daily routine may be to order parts or to stock your trucks, online reviews should be part of that as well.

Lots of citations

A citation in simple terms is a mention or listing of your company information online, typically citations are also directory sites, and social media sites, your N.A.P information needs to be consistent across all sites.

What does N.A.P stand for?

Name

Address

Phone number

All those should be consistent across all citations. So, capitalization and spelling matters. If you use an uppercase letter in one citation you want to use it in all the others.

Let's say your company address is 123mainstreet. If you spell out the word "street," you want to keep it consistent and spell it out across all the other citations. So, don't use the abbreviation "ST" for street on some and then spell it out for others.

All those "little" details can affect the rankings of your Website.

You want to have a solid link profile across the web.

Action Items:

Check for Duplicate Content if your website isn't ranking.

Create an individual city page for all cities in your service area and also for all services that you offer.

Sign up for a Google Webmaster Account.

Check for low quality or irrelevant links pointing to your site, if you find any consider disavowing them.

Make sure your overall SEO strategy includes: On Page SEO, Off Page SEO and User Experience SEO.

Sign up for a Google Analytics Accounts to see the user metrics such as click through rate (CTR), Bounce Rate etc.

Do some keyword research using the Google Keyword Planner.

Consider leveraging multimedia especially video, will help keep consumers on your website longer.

Use reviews to improve user experience.

Add the main keyword that you want to target to the Title of the page and the H1 tag.

Create a high converting meta description once your site is on page one to increase your click through rate.

Write blog posts or articles on an ongoing basis to keep your site updated and to rank for more keywords.

Sign up for a Google My Business account and directory websites like Yelp and Yellow Pages.

Set up a Google My Business listing if you don't already have one, this will help both your map

Chapter 8 - Why You Should Consider Yelp For Appliance Repair Leads

Before we discuss this topic, let me first say, I am not necessarily endorsing that you pay for ads from Yelp, because their advertising can be expensive, however, it's worth testing depending on your monthly advertising budget. But by simply getting a free listing with them, you can start to get free appliance repair leads.

Recently, a study was conducted to find out the trust level of people on reviews given by users on websites. It was found that more than 75 percent of people trusted these online reviews. There are many online review websites that can influence the hiring of an appliance repair company decision of their users. One such popular site is Yelp. The site has more than 125 million unique visitors every month. It is one of the most powerful review sites that is used by both young and old. If you are a part of the appliance repair industry, chances are, your potential customers are using Yelp, and there might already be several reviews of your business on the site.

One of the reasons why most businesses want their business to be listed on Yelp is because the site has an impressive array of users. Also, the majority of users are in the age group of 25-34, which is the target audience of most appliance repair companies. Here are some important stats you must be aware of when listing your appliance service business on Yelp.

Profile of the Audience
Female – 53.85%
    Male – 46.15%
    Married – 45.4%
    Married with Children – 36.2%
    Attended Graduate School or College – 72.2%
Age Composition of Users
    18-24 – 13.2%

25-34 – 25.2%
35-44 – 18.1%
45-54 – 19.0%
55-64 – 15%
Above 65 – 9.7%

Another interesting fact you must be aware of is that more than 37 percent of the users have a household income in excess of $100,000. Even more important is the fact that most people who use Yelp are those who are planning to make an immediate purchase of a product or service. In fact, nearly 40 percent of Yelp users visit the website of the searched business within 24 hours.

Therefore, it is important that have a great rating on their website. Also, a decent amount of reviews will improve your listing.

Chapter 9 - How To Get Yelp Working For Your Business

Before you take steps to list your appliance repair business on Yelp, it is important to check if your business is already listed on Yelp. A simple search will help you in checking the status of your listing. Even if you never used Yelp, chances are, your business is listed on the site. This is because the users create most content you find on the site. That is why you should immediately visit the site to check out if your business is listed.

Searching for your appliance repair company listing on Yelp is easy. All you have to do is put the name of your company on their search bar, select the city and state, and click on search. If the name of your business pops up, it indicates that your business is listed. If your business is listed, all you have to do is select the "Claim your Business" option. When you claim your business, you will be able to update your contact details, add photos, check the reviews given by customers, and get all possible information on your target audience.

To claim your business, all you have to do is enter your name, address, contact number, and the password. Once you enter these details, select agree to the Terms of Service of Yelp. After you have completed these formalities, the claim process will be completed.

Adding Your Business

If you find that your business is not listed on Yelp, you will have to add the details of your business manually. To complete this process, you must visit the "Add your Business" section of the site. You must then enter the following details:

Name of your Business

Complete Address
City, State, and the Zip Code
Phone Number(s)
Website Address
Business Hours
Important Business Categories
Email Address

Once these details are submitted, Yelp will review your submission. This can take a few days. Once your listing is approved, you will receive an email confirmation.

Fill out your Business Page

Filling out the details on your appliance repair business page will help in providing prospective customers all essential information about your company. Since Yelp is targeted at locals who are looking for information about local business, leaving out essential details of your business, can turn-off potential customers.

So, what is some of the information that customers are looking for? These include:

Complete address
Website Address
Hours of Operation
Price Range of your Products or Service
Photos
Parking Information
If you accept credit cards
Parking Availability for walk-in Customers
Turnaround Time
Products your service and repair
Repair and Service Warranty

You also have an option to choose the items you want to display, so select each option carefully. Make sure you include as many details about your company as possible to make it easy for people to contact you and use your service.

This step is extremely important even if your company is already listed on Yelp. You must make sure that all details on the website are correct and take steps to revise incorrect details.

An important point to note is that the users can easily modify your appliance repair company information. So, make sure this information is updated regularly. Even though the information must go through the moderator first, you must still keep track of these changes.

Using Yelp can help your business in several ways. When you analyze the demographics of people who are checking out your business listing, you gain insight into who your target audience is. This information will help in promoting your business as you can design services, products, ads, and content to suit their needs.

When the user clicks through your website, bookmarks your listing, calls for more information on your business, or checks into your business, you will be given the following information about the user:

Name
Link to their profile on Yelp
Age
Gender
Home City

The user can turn the above information off in their privacy settings, but if they don't, you will have some valuable information to understanding your target audience.

Chapter 10 - Add Craigslist To Your Marketing Plan

I can hear some of you already saying "Craigslist, C'mon" I know, but hear me out, yes, Craigslist may have low-quality leads, that are price shoppers and are looking for free diagnostics, but this isn't always the case, quality leads can come from Craigslist. From my experience, it is the preferred choice for property managers, if they need to find an appliance repair company is Craigslist, now how many of you wouldn't mind working with more property managers? I'm sure most of you wouldn't, which I why I am including Craigslist in this book, but since it's no longer FREE to post your appliance repair ads, make sure you test and track it to see if it's worth the investment.

How to Post an Ad on Craigslist?

Just in case you are new to using Craigslist, or you just dismissed using it because you heard all the horror stories, I wanted to include a step by step process to get up and running with your first Ad.

1. Visit Craigslist.org and create an account.
2. Once you are logged in, on the left menu, you will see an option to "Post To Classifieds."
3. Next, your type of posting is "Service Offered."
4. Pick the category "Household Services" or "Skilled Trade Services," you can test each category to see which one works best for your area.
5. Choose the location nearest to your service area.
6. Now it's time to create your ad.
7. Choose a title and description for your ad. "Specific Location" is not a required field. Don't choose the option to "use this email address as my reply to" as you will get a lot of spam.

8. Click "Continue"
9. Review ad on the next page and if it is okay, type in the word verification and click "Continue" to submit the post

Tips for Writing Titles and Descriptions

You must write an attention-grabbing title, which should include your city in your title, this is the first step to making your ad stand out. Include at least one keyword phrase, which in your case the best one you could use is Appliance Repair.

When you are writing the description, include information that will be important to the consumer, like "Fast Same Day Service" and don't forget to include your call to action (specifically what you want them to do), from our testing we prefer to just include a phone number, instead of having them go to a website.

You have the option to do image or text ads, start simply, text ads work, no need to complicate things. Later on, when you feel like experimenting, you can look into creating some image ads and test them.

Avoid Getting Banned - Craigslist Restrictions

Craigslist is mostly monitored by the users, what that means is your competitor can flag your ad as spam, and believe me a lot of them do, so that their ads can show up at the top, this is not a practice that I recommend, instead what this means is you may need to post multiple ads, and I just wanted to bring it to your attention just in case you run into this problem. It's also not a bad idea to read through Craigslist Terms of Use.

Chapter 11 – Pay Per Lead And NOT Per Click With Google's Local Service Ads

Google Local Service Ads And How It Works?

Google is the #1 search engine, and for a few years now, they have put priority on delivering local results for their end users. End user or consumer experience is very important to them, that is why when they realized that more consumers are using their smartphones or mobile devices to search online, they developed voice search and in 2018 they moved from a desktop index to a mobile-first index.

Google pays close attention to consumer wants and needs, after all, consumers are responsible for turning them into a Multi-Billion Dollar Empire!

They also understand that when a consumer searches online for an appliance repair company, there are some concerns that consumers have and at the top of the consumer's list is when they hire an appliance repair technician to fix their appliances, who exactly are they letting into their home?

You can do a search on YouTube for "appliance repair scams," and you will find a few videos, from news channels across the U.S., where consumers were taken advantage of by an appliance repairman.

To help solve this problem, Google has now introduced Google Local Service Ads (LSA) for the appliance repair industry. Now to be fair I don't think Google did this only for the consumers, I think they also saw how much revenue lead generation companies like HomeAdvisor (another Billion Dollar company) is making and saw it as an opportunity to compete in the lead generation space.

That doesn't mean their Local Service Ads program works like HomeAdvisors', but they do have a qualification process that is similar to HomeAdvisor where they do require licenses, insurance, and a background check.

When a consumer now searches in a city where LSA is available, they will see a few trusted professionals and these LSA ads show up above the regular Google Ads section, and these LSA ads include reviews, ratings, hours and contact number.

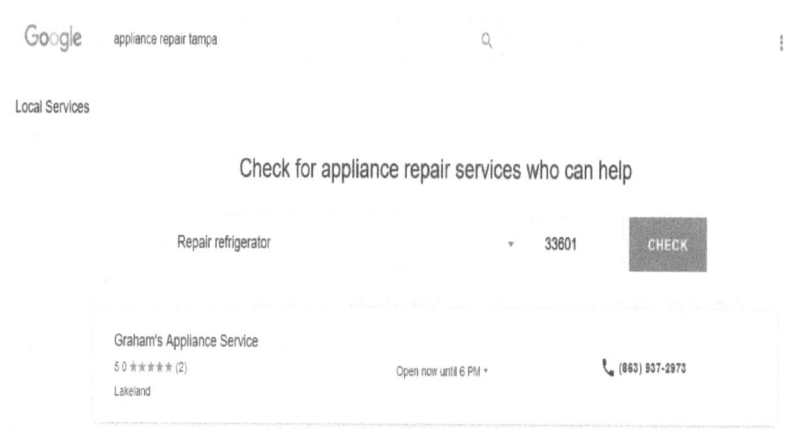

Google wants to make sure they are connecting consumers to the right appliance service advertiser, so LSA ads go one step further than traditional Google Ads. So, when the consumer clicks on the appliance repair company listing, they are then prompted to confirm the type of appliance repair job that they are looking for and their location. If your appliance repair company does service the appliance that the consumer needs to be fixed and your company services the location of the consumer, then you will be matched to the consumers, and from there the consumer can check out your reviews, ratings, and qualifications before calling your business.

If your business is NOT a good fit for a particular appliance service job or if it's outside your service area, then Google will not charge you for that appliance repair job lead, and instead, they will connect the consumer with a better option by showing them more Local Service Ads to better match their search criteria.

LSA will display on mobile, tablet and desktop searches, but the reach will be greater than with regular Google Ads. LSA is now part of Google Assistant's responses for relevant voice searches, in which the Google Assistant will ask the consumer their location and what appliance repair service they are looking for, to better match them to the right appliance repair company.

When we do our appliance repair keyword research, it's not uncommon for us to find new keywords that include "ok google" if you have the Google Home device, an android smartphone or tablet then you are probably already familiar with seeing "ok google", but just in case you don't have any of those or have just never heard of "ok google," that phrase is used to activate the Google Assistant feature. In our keyword research, we will see things like "ok google find me an appliance repair company near me."

What Cities Are Google Local Service Ads Available In?

As of December 2018, Google Local Service ads are available for appliance repair companies in the following markets:

- • Atlanta
- • Dallas
- • Houston
- • Los Angeles
- • Minneapolis-St. Paul
- • Orlando
- • Philadelphia
- • Phoenix
- • San Diego
- • Tampa
- • Washington, DC

Benefits to Google's Local Service Ads

Probably the most important one for appliance repair companies is that they Pay per Lead – not Click!

If you currently use or have used Google Ads in the past, then I don't have to tell you what a pain it is, for clicks when the consumer doesn't call or if it's a bad lead like a warranty or parts call, when you don't do warranty work or sell parts.

LSA will help appliance service business owners to connect with the right appliance repair job leads, which will help with the problem of getting low-quality appliance repair leads that typically happen with regular Google Ads, as consumers can sometimes use comprehensive search terms, such as "appliance repair" when they are really just looking to buy a specific appliance part.

Or another example would be when consumer calls from their mobile phone and they work and live in 2 different cities, Google will show them an Ad that is based on their mobile phone GPS location, which could be location you service but because they live in a completely different city which is where they want the appliance fixed, then it could be too far outside your service area.

With LSA, you will only pay for valid leads and depending on your service area and job type, you will pay around $26 per appliance repair job lead. If you do get a lead that you think is not valid such as one of your competitors calling you, poor matches, such as being outside your service area or a telemarketing lead, you can start a dispute to get a credit.

The Google Guaranteed - Gain Trust For Your Appliance Repair Company

There is no question that consumers trust Google; this is exactly why Search Engine Optimization and Google Ads has been the best ways for appliance repair businesses to get new appliance job leads for the past few years. If your appliance service company shows up on the first page of Google, then in a consumer's mind, they assume you must be a good company.

Google has leveraged this consumer trust with LSA, and now consumers will not only see your appliance service business on the first page, but they will see you at the very top, and the Ad will have a green checkmark along with "Google Guaranteed."

> **Vision Appliance Repair**
> 5.0 ★★★★★ · See reviews
> ✅ GOOGLE GUARANTEED
> Serves Washington
> (202) 795-5207
> Open now

Not only will the Google Guaranteed help you to grab the attention of more consumers in an already busy Search Engine Results Page, but your appliance repair company will get an additional benefit of having a very powerful endorsement from Google. This endorsement is much more than just Google backing your company by reputation, but also the Google Guaranteed is in place to protect customers who may have not been happy with the completed job, with a lifetime cap coverage of $2000.

Show Off Your Positive Ratings & Reviews

For regular Google Ads, you can no longer add review extensions, but with LSA you can include existing customer reviews to help you gain more trust from potential prospects, and this is one way to ensure that your past customer reviews show up in the Google Search Engine Results Page.

Paid Search Ads – Expand Your Reach With LSA

LSA show up at the very top of the search, above the Paid Ads section, Map results and the organic listings. LSA wasn't designed to replace any of these sections; this is because, in addition to creating another revenue stream for Google, they know that some consumers will want to still take a look at your website, before making a final decision on whether you are the best appliance repair business in town. However, we know that being at the top of Google is prime online real estate and with LSA being in this prime location and with the help of good customer reviews, these factors will help to convert more prospects into customers once they get a chance to check out your appliance repair website.

Why Your Appliance Repair Company Needs To Be Included In Voice Searches?

Isn't it a lot easier to just talk into your phone to send a text message, instead of typing it in?

I know I don't have to tell appliance repair technicians this, as they are probably all doing it already, one hand working on the appliance, the other one using their mobile phone, it's how appliance service technicians get things done and efficiently. Google Assistant powers over 400 million devices, as Google has caught on to the trend that customers prefer to simply talk into their phone than to open a browser and type a search query into the search engines. Voice search is now responsible for about 20% of online searches and with LSA, you can guarantee that your appliance repair company will be included in Voice Searches for local appliance repair companies.

No Keywords or Ads to Manage – Stop The Madness!

Ok, so you can probably tell I am a big fan of Shark Tank, which is where I got that "Stop The Madness" line, thanks to Kevin "Mr. Wonderful" O'Leary.

One of the challenges with traditional Google Ads is that it requires a lot of maintenance and testing different ads to find the best converting ones and finding new keyword ideas, seem to be an ever-ending task. And if you weren't managing your ads and keywords, then it may have been one of the reasons you didn't see success with Google Ads in the past.

I have some good news for you!

With LSA there are no ads or keywords to manage, instead LSA will automatically get trigged when a consumer types in any appliance repair related keyword, and there are thousands of appliance repair related search terms, so no matter if its as broad as "Appliance Repair" or as narrow as "my fridge is not cooling," Google will use the information in your business profile to determine if they should show your LSA ads.

How To Get Started With Google's Local Service Ads?

Find Out If You Are Eligible

LSA is not currently available in all cities, at least as of January 2019, so depending on when you are reading this it may or may not be available in your city, however, you can find out by going here:

https://adwords.google.com/localservices/signup/eligibility

If after filling out the information at that link and you find out that LSA has not rolled out to your city yet, don't worry, it will be soon, as Google is expanding LSA into new cities at a very fast pace, and you have the option to sign up so you can get notified as soon as it becomes available in your city.

If on the other hand, you are eligible, then you will be guided through the steps to get your account set up, so you can start and manage your Local Service Ads. Currently, LSA is managed in a completely separate account from what you may be using for Google Ads Express or traditional Google Ads (AdWords), so you will need to set up a new account to give LSA a try.

Set Up Your Business Profile

It's important that you set up your business profile accurately and completely because your profile is going to determine the types of appliance repair jobs that your appliance company gets matched to. So let's say you don't want microwave repair jobs from LSA, then don't list it in your profile, just because you can fix microwaves doesn't mean you have to list it, since you are paying for appliance repair leads from LSA, then you may want to just focus on the jobs where you have more profit margins like high-end appliance repair or refrigerator repairs. The same would apply to your service area, if it includes low-income areas, then you may want to leave those out and just add the mid to higher income areas that are within your service area.

Here are a few things you can edit within your business profile:

- Business hours
- Weekly budget
- Job types
- Service areas

There is also an option for you to add things that will highlight your profile, don't skip this step as it's an important one, these highlights will improve the conversion rate of your LSA ads, as they show on both your business detail page as well as alongside your LSA.

Here are some ideas of things you will want to highlight in your Appliance Repair Local Service Ads:

- Locally Owned and Operated

- Military Discounts
- 24 Hour Service
- Same Day Service

These highlights are optional; however, it's also important because it will help consumers to choose your appliance repair business over your competition.

Include Your License & Insurance Information

You will need to prove that you are insured and licensed to be able to run LSA and to earn your Google Guarantee badge. So, make sure your documents are up to date before submitting your professional licenses and your general liability insurance paperwork.

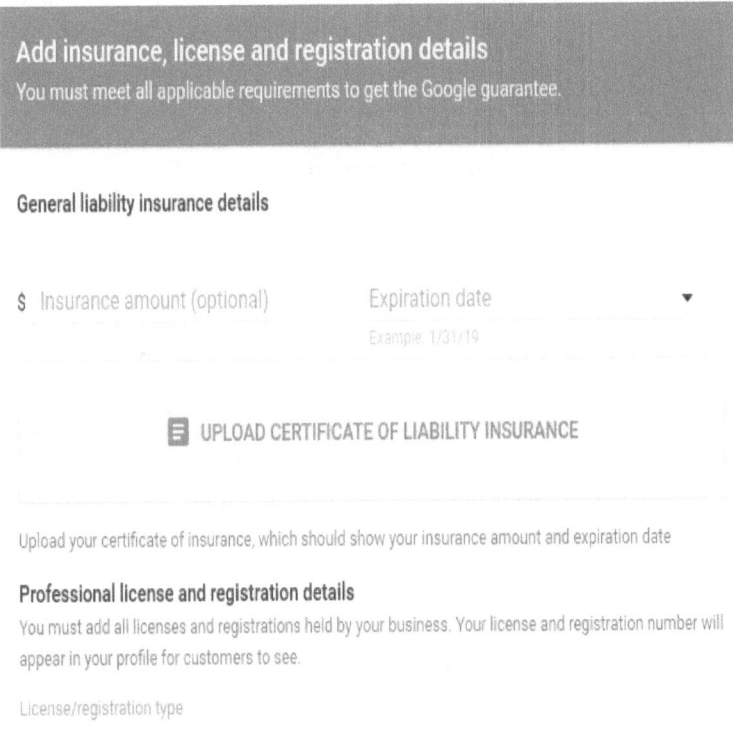

Submit Your Background Check

Before Google starts to send appliance repair technicians into consumers' homes, they are going to want to make sure the consumers are safe and that they can rely on LSA appliance repair advertisers who are covered by the Google Guarantee. This is why appliance repair companies and their technicians will be required to pass a background check.

Pinkerton is the company that Google has partnered with to do this, and there is no cost to complete the background checks.

How To Manage Your Appliance Repair Leads?

Once you set up your appliance repair business profile and it's complete, you will be able to start running your Local Service Ads to get new appliance service leads in your local service area. You can manage and view your new appliance repair jobs leads here:

google.com/HomeServices/inbox

Once you are in your dashboard, look for the "Leads" tab in the drop-down menu in the upper right corner of your screen. There is also an LSA app for IOS and Android phones, so you can manage your inbound leads on your mobile device.

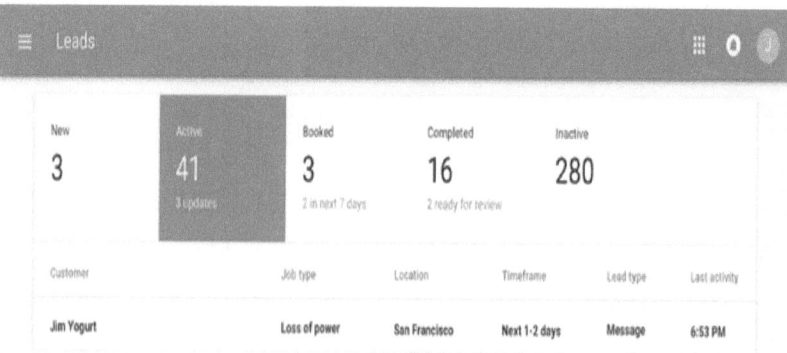

It's important to note that all leads are not booked jobs, and that is why you want to make sure that all inbound leads get followed up on and in a timely manner. You can click on an individual lead within your dashboard to view all the details for that lead, such as location, job type and listen to the call recording.

After reviewing the details of the leads, you will see 3 different options for you to use, to follow up on these hot prospects:

- **Call** the lead on the phone number they provided.
- **Reply** to the lead by text or email.
- **Decline** the lead. When you decline a job, the customer will be notified of this, and it will be removed from your dashboard, you also have the option to recover declined jobs if you declined it in error.

You also have the option to label your leads as booked, to help better keep track of your return on investment and you can use this feature to also do the following:

- Collect customer reviews
- Send confirmation emails
- Schedule jobs

Budget Management

You will have the ability to adjust your LSA budget from within your business profile. You have full control of your budget, and how much you want to spend, so you can lower or raise your average weekly budget. However, when it comes to budget, LSA and regular Google Ads have something in common, and that is even though you set your weekly budget at a specific amount, Google can spend more or less than that amount on a weekly basis, but it won't exceed your total monthly budget.

Keep in mind that since you are paying per lead with LSA and not per click when you decrease or increase your budget, you will see a direct impact on the amount or appliance service job leads that you receive.

When you set up your account, you will see an option to choose the amount of leads you want to receive, if you are wondering what a good amount of leads to start with would be, I would recommend 20 leads per week and that will give you a good indication of how things work and what type of ROI you can expect to see with LSA.

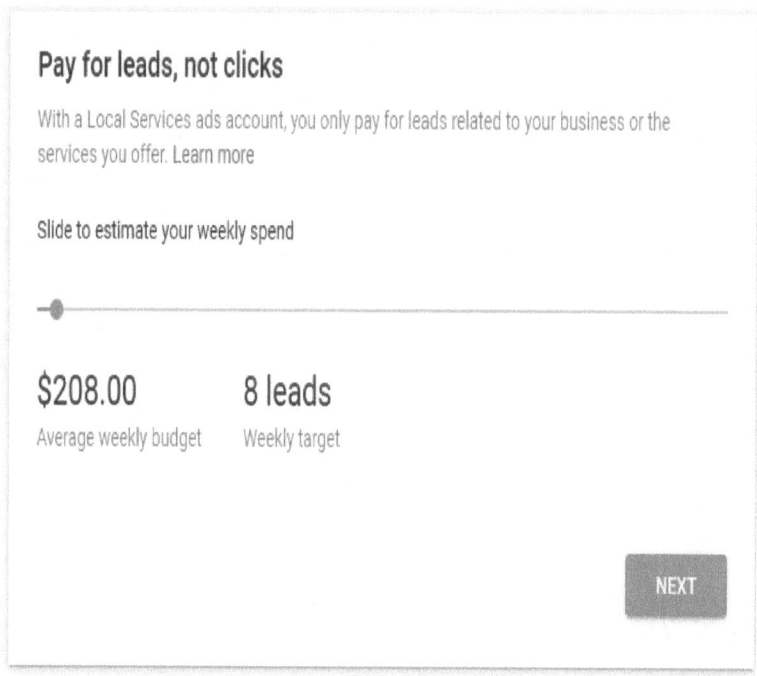

And since your LSA budget is separate from your AdWords budget, then if you are running ads on both platforms, then you will want to specify a budget for both since you will now have combined costs of both platforms.

How Is Ad Rank Calculated For Local Service Ads?

There was already limited space on the search engine results page even before the introduction of LSA, and currently, the setup is that 3 local service ads will show up on a desktop computer, 2 on a mobile device and 1 for Google Assistant. And just like with regular AdWords if you want your ads to show up first, you will want to ensure that your ad has an ad rank that is high.

You will NOT have to worry about these ranking factors, however, with LSA:

- Landing page
- Ad relevance
- Click through rates

Instead, this is how the Ad Rank for your Local Service Ads are calculated:

- How close your appliance repair business is to the consumer's location.
- The number of reviews you have and the total review score.
- How responsive you are to inbound lead requests and inquires.
- Hours of operation.
- Complaints – whether you receive complaints, the seriousness of the complaint and if you get repeated complaints.

Don't Forget Reviews

I have been saying for years now, how important reviews are becoming for appliance service companies and why it should part of your everyday business plan. That's why it is no surprise to me, that reviews are an important ranking factor for LSA, so make sure you ask all satisfied customers to leave you a review to help with improving your LSA rankings but to also improve the overall online reputation of your company. The good news is that Google has made it very easy to use the LSA platform to contact customers that scheduled their appointment through the LSA platform to ask them for their review.

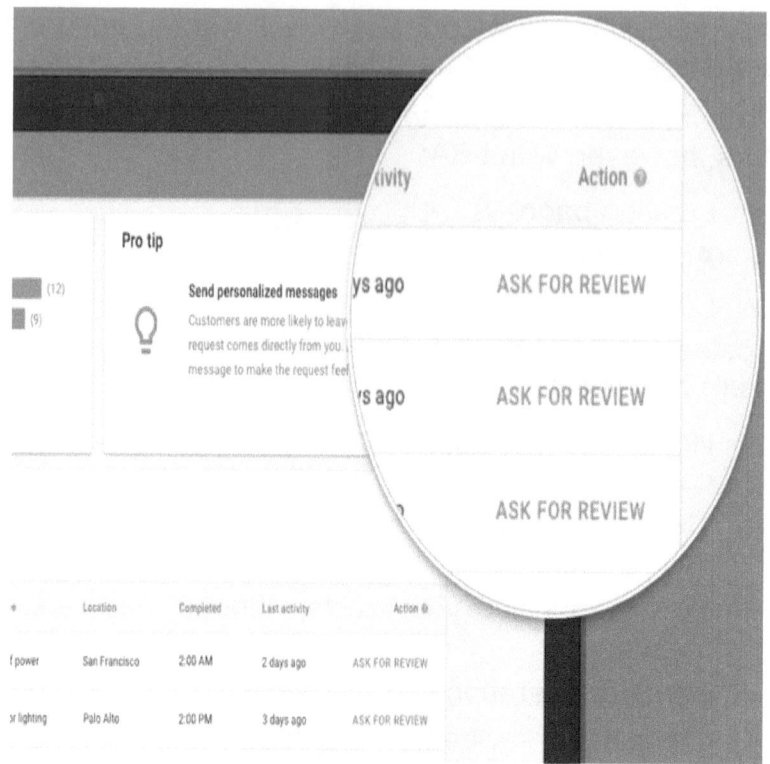

Once you are logged into your LSA dashboard, go to the "Reviews" tab, where you will see a list of jobs you completed, and from there you can directly ask the customer for a review. If you want to increase the likelihood of customers that leave reviews, then try personalizing the message to them.

Frequently Asked Questions

What Is A Valid Lead With LSA?

Valid leads can occur when local consumers find your Appliance Repair Local Services ad on Google and one of the following occurs:

- You receive an email or text message from the lead.
- You receive a voicemail message from the lead.
- You speak to the lead on the phone.

When there is a missed call (even if the lead doesn't leave a voicemail), and if you respond to the missed call or voicemail with a call, email or a text message, where you either leave a voicemail or speak directly with the customer.

If you don't get charged for the lead, you'll see the following message in your dashboard:

What types of leads are considered INVALID?

If you were charged for a bad lead, you could dispute the charge in your account.

Here is a list "bad leads" that are eligible for a credit:

Appliance repair job requested is not listed on your company profile.

- Lead's location is outside your service area.
- Not a consumer (for example solicitations, telemarketing or wrong number).
- Not a human (automated telemarketing calls).
- If you got billed for the same lead within a 15 day period.
- You received a lead with invalid contact information, so you had no way of following up.

If you got charged for a lead that you think is bad, but it doesn't fall into the categories listed above, then you can always contact LSA support and explain the situation at 866-2-GOOGLE.

Although you have up to 60 days to dispute a lead, you also have the option to dispute the charges within your dashboard immediately. Before Google issues a credit, they will have a support agent to listen to the call recordings to verify that one of the above and approved reasons apply.

Examples of valid appliance repair leads that you shouldn't expect to get a credit for:

•Lead came in after your normal business hours.

•Lead wanted advice over the phone to troubleshoot their appliance.

•Lead called back to cancel after scheduling the service call.

•Lead was only researching prices for service call or to fix the appliance.

•Lead didn't return your message or call.

•You have refrigerator repair service listed on your profile, but you don't service all types or brands of refrigerators.

Do both owners and appliance service technicians have to do a background and drug test?

No, drug tests are not part of the on boarding process, but a background check is.

How are the top 3 appliance repair advertisers chosen?

Proximity to the consumer who is searching for appliance repair or related search is the biggest factor, and the 2nd biggest is reviews. However, it is important to note, that if you are not logged into your dashboard and following up with leads, in what Google would consider to be within a timely manner, your ads will not show as often in the top 3. Also, if you are turning down a lot of leads, Google will start to assume that you can't handle the current volume of leads and display your ad less.

Do all technicians have to do the background check?

If you are running appliance repair ads and have 5 techs, all 5 techs will need to be verified with a background check.

Why isn't the Google Guaranteed badge not showing on my Ad?

Once you go through the verification process (i.e., all background checks for all techs, professional license & general liability insurance submitted and approved), the Google Guaranteed badge should show whenever your ads are running. However, if you turn off your ads, then it will not show while the ads are off. Yes, that means Google still shows your ad even when you turn them off, but you won't be charged for any customer requests while the Google Guarantee badge is not showing.

If LSA is not available in some zip codes within my service area, can I still sign up for the zip codes that LSA is available in?

Yes.

Conclusion:

Like all sources of advertising, whether online or offline, it's worth testing to see if it will work for your appliance repair company and since Local Service Ads already have the tracking features in place, you will be able to decide if it's right for you. If you have tried Google AdWords in the past and it didn't work for you, it doesn't mean LSA is also not a good fit, and if you compare both LSA and Google AdWords simply because they are Google products, you are not comparing apples to apples.

This also doesn't mean you should replace AdWords with LSA. If you are having success with AdWords, I would recommend you figure out how many clicks it's taking you to get a phone call or a good lead, once you know that number, you can then try LSA and see how they compare. For some appliance repair companies, they will find LSA provides a better ROI, while some may see that AdWords will work out better and others will like both.

We highly recommend that if you want a consistent flow of incoming leads to your appliance repair business, then you have to use multiple sources of advertising or lead generation

Action Items:

- Consider signing up for and testing Google's Local Service Ads if it's available in your area.
- Test at least 20 leads can calculate your ROI from there.
- If you get a good ROI, follow the recommendations in this chapter to improve your quality score.

Chapter 12 – Convert MORE Of Your Website's Visitors Into Callers!

Think of your website as the hub, everything that you're doing with online marketing comes back to the website.

If you're doing social media marketing, SEO, local directory advertising like Yelp or Yellow pages and paid search advertising like Google AdWords, when the consumer clicks on any of your ads or content, they will lead back to your website.

This is why website conversion is so important, and just in case you're not familiar with that term, and what exactly **website conversion is, it's getting a consumer that visits your appliance service website to take a specific action**, which is to either call or to fill out a form on your website.

You could have many consumers visiting your appliance repair website, but if you don't have the right conversion elements, it could be one of the reasons why your website is not actually getting you the leads that you are hoping it would generate for you. So that's what we're going to really focus on in this chapter and give you a few tips to help improve the conversion rate on your website.

So why is website conversion so important?

Let's look at two scenarios.

Why conversion is SO important?

SENARIO 1:	SENARIO 2:
500 Visitors per month	500 Visitors per month
5% Conversion	15% Conversion
25 Calls / Leads	75 Calls / Leads
30% Conversion	30% Conversion
7 Booked Jobs	22 Booked Jobs
$150 Average Transaction	$150 Average Transaction
$1,050	$3,300

Scenario one is that you have 500 visitors per month.

Let's assume that you have a current conversion rate of 5%. That would give you 25 calls or leads.

And let's say you have a 30% conversion on the phone.

Now we're talking about when the customer calls in; the 30% conversion is rate at which your appliance repair company can turn those phone calls into scheduled appointments.

With a 30% conversion rate, you will have 7 booked jobs.

And let's assume that your average completed appliance repair is worth $150 to your appliance service company, for some of you the average job could be worth more or less, and you can adjust that number accordingly when you try to figure out the actual conversion rate for your appliance repair business.

The 7 booked jobs will be worth $1,050 in revenue to your appliance repair business.

Now let's look at scenario number two, we're going to try and keep everything the same.

Same 500 visitors per month.

But what we want to improve is the website conversion rate. So instead of the 5% conversion rate, let's say we get you up to a 15% conversion rate.

Now your phone calls went from 25 calls to 75 calls.

Same conversion on the phone of 30%.

Now we have 22 booked jobs instead of 7.

Same average repair value or $150.

Now we just brought in $3,300 for your appliance repair business, instead of $1,050.

And keep in mind, we didn't get any more people to come to our website than what we normally do. All we did was to improve the conversion rate on the website.

Hopefully, it's starting to make a lot more sense now why the conversion rate of your appliance service website is so important.

**Sometimes it's not that you need more leads to get more appliance service business to come in.
Sometimes you just need to improve the conversion rate.**

In the above example, we improved the conversion rate of just the website, which went from 5% to 15%. But another conversion rate that we could improve on is the incoming phone call conversion rate.

Hopefully, this picture of conversion rate optimization is getting a little bit clearer now.

And that's why I wanted just to give you some type of illustration, because sometimes that helps clear things up a bit.

Now that you understand the importance of optimizing your conversion rates, you're probably wondering, how exactly does an appliance repair business owner do it?

That's what we're going to talk about next.

9 critical elements to improve the conversion of your website.

1. The first one is that you want to speak the language of your target market.

Your target market is the largest segment of consumers that actually call you and includes your existing customer base. If you were to look at all the customers that have hired your appliance repair company over the last 6 months or last year, and if you could make a list of all of them, you would start to notice certain commonalities between each of them.

You would see a pattern that arises from that, such as a particular age range or whether they are mostly males or females that hire you.

It's important to know such details, and I'm going to show you why as the training goes on.

You should know the fears and frustrations consumers have when it comes to hiring an appliance service company. You can use that information to communicate to them, why they should choose your appliance repair business over your local competition.

2. **Be real with them** – What I mean by that is, you want to have authentic images of your team on the homepage or your website. Consumers want to see the owners and technicians.

3. **Use video and other multimedia elements** – To engage consumers.

You should have different elements for the different types of consumers to engage with your appliance repair company.

- Senior citizens are just looking for a phone number when they visit your site.
- Millennials are looking for a way they can text or email, as they prefer not to speak on the phone.

A welcome video on a website is great. Having a video on each page of your website that explains the different appliance repair services that you offer would be ideal.

4. **Leverage social proof** – Showcase your online reviews from existing customers prominently on the homepage or all the pages of your website. Some tools that you can use to do this is birdeye.com and reviewbuzz.com.
5. **Get the basics in order** – Phone number should be in the upper right-hand corner of your website. And it should be big and bold; you could even put it in a red or yellow font color to let it stand out more.

The reason for this is, when consumers come to your website, there are a lot of studies done that show that a consumer's eyes first go to the upper right-hand corner.

And most consumers, when they need to hire an appliance repair company, they're not trying to do a whole lot of research. The number one thing they're looking for on an appliance repair website is that phone number. So, make it very easy for them to find it.

Ensure that there's also a web form that consumers can fill out.

You should have some type of form on your website that someone can just put in their basic information:

- Name
- Phone number

- Problem that you're having

Some consumers are not going to be able to call, as they work during the week and are not able to speak on the phone during regular business hours.

If they could simply just fill out a form and schedule the appointment, it makes things a lot easier for them.

- **Add credibility and authority symbols to your website** – If you're a member of the better business bureau or Angie's list, you should add those logos to your website. People recognize these big names, and you can leverage them to build credibility and authority for your appliance repair company.
6. **Have a clear call to action on each page** – That speaks to your ideal customers and tells them exactly what to do next. If you're not familiar with a call to action, basically you're just telling the consumer what action you want them to take.

Examples of a call to action are:

- call us now
- call us today
- fill out the form.
7. **Use special offers and coupons** that match each service that they are in need of. Coupons are a great way to get consumers to call. If you're apprehensive about using coupons because it's going to reduce your revenue, coupons are shown to increase revenue. The reason is because you will start to get more people call because everyone loves to save money.

So, you will get a larger volume or service request, and even though you may make a smaller profit, with the larger volume of service requests, it makes up for it.

And don't forget about the repeat jobs you will get from existing customers and the referrals. Those more than make up for the amount of money you may have lost by offering a coupon.

If you're against coupons, I really encourage you to rethink about using it to get more business.

8. **Make sure your website is mobile optimized** – with an easy click to call function.

One quick and easy way to check if your appliance repair website is mobile friendly is to just go to the browser on your phone and try to pull up your website.

It's also good to look at how the website displays on both an android phone and an iPhone. Because they will display differently on the different phones and you want to make sure that it actually displays correctly on the different mobile devices.

More people are using their mobile devices to access the search engines, and this trend is only growing. 70 to 80 percent of the people that visit your website are probably doing so from a mobile device.

Not only should your website display correctly, but also make sure the phone number is at the top, and there should also be a button that consumers can just tap actually to call your appliance service business.

They shouldn't have to memorize your phone number to actually type it in, because they're probably not going to. That's too much work! They're probably not going to do that. So, what you need to provide them is a click to call button, that when tapped, your number shows up and from there they just need to click on send or call on the mobile device.

If there's one thing to take away from this chapter, it is to **make sure your website is mobile friendly**. That's because **if it's not, you're losing customers every day**.

9. **Consider leveraging live chat** - This is probably a little bit better than the web form that we discussed earlier. This is because with live chat, consumers can just type in what they need to do, and they can

get an instant response from your appliance repair company. So, if you have the staff available to actually handle a live chat, it's something that you should consider implementing.

If you can see your ideal customers through their eyes, then you can better sell them what they want to buy.

You may have heard something similar to this or another similar saying, that if you really want to understand what someone's going through, you have to put yourself in that person's shoes to understand.

It's important to understand the fears and the frustrations of consumers that need appliance repair, because then if you can better understand your potential customers, you can close more and schedule more jobs for your appliance repair company.

Who is your ideal customer?

Let's take a look at some demographic information in the image below:

- **Demographics**
    - Home Owner
    - 35+ years old
    - Typically female occasionally male
    - Married with 2-3 kids
    - Head of household
    - $65K+ Annual Household Income
    - Family oriented
    - Reliable
    - Easily frustrated
    - Likes to please people & expects the same in return
    - Not handy
    - Likes gardening, crafting & arts

These are just some examples of things that you want to look out for:

- Are they homeowners or renters?
- What age group are they in?
- Is it typically female or male that usually hire your appliance repair company?
- Are they single or married?

- Do they have kids, and if so, how many kids?

These are just some examples of what you want to look at to figure out the demographics of your ideal customer.

Now let's talk about the pains and frustrations

The pain and frustration is that their appliance stopped working.

If the dishwasher broke, now they have to start washing dishes by hand.

If the washing machine is not working, now they have to go to the laundromat to get that done.

All these things are big inconveniences to a consumer.

Another frustration is that when they do call an appliance repair company, they can't get anyone on the phone.

Especially if they left a voicemail message, and an hour has gone by with no one calling them back from the appliance service company.

It's frustrating because consumers are busy, and they don't want to spend a lot of time calling around town to find an appliance repair company, and they need their appliance problem resolved right away.

Appliance repair is an emergency industry

So, consumers that need appliance repair are expecting to get the repair completed fast, as in today, so most are looking for same day service but depending on the appliance some consumers may wait for next day service.

Additional fears when it comes to choosing an appliance repair company:

- They worry about getting ripped off by the appliance repair company or getting overcharged for the repair.

- They worry about paying too much for something they could have gotten done cheaper somewhere else.
- They don't want to invest a lot of money into an appliance that's not even worth fixing.
- Having their home damaged by faulty workmanship.
- Having a technician come in and cause additional damage to their home
- Having to wait around all day for the tech to arrive at their home.

That's why they like shorter appointment windows and why doing a 30-minute call ahead is very much appreciated by consumers.

Some appliance repair companies will overbook their schedule because they have issues with consumers cancelling appointments, and as a result, some consumers are left waiting all day for a technician, and no one shows up.

- They are sometimes inconvenienced trying to coordinate with the tech. So sometimes what happens here is that some appliance repair companies don't offer service after 5 pm or on the weekends. Now for someone that works during the week, they now have to take a day off, and then in some cases, they don't even get paid. So, you can just imagine how frustrated the consumer would be if after doing all that the appliance repair technician doesn't show up.
- The invoice or the cost of the repair will be more than they can afford

Now let's talk about messaging that works.

These are things that you want to have on your website, and this also applies if you're doing any type of paid online advertising like Yelp or Google AdWords. These are all elements that you can incorporate in your message to get more consumers to call your appliance service business.

- Same day service
- Emergency service
- Short appointment windows.
- Straightforward or upfront pricing
- Satisfaction guaranteed.

They want to know that if there's an issue after the repair, that they're not going to have to pay the technician to come and fix the same problem again.

They want to know that customer service is important to your company and that you stand behind your work, with some type of warranty or guarantee.

- Trustworthy appliance service technicians coming into their homes.
- Experienced technician

The question now is, based on everything that we just covered, is your appliance repair company website set up to convert visitors into callers?

Action Items:

- **Add real authentic images of your team** to the homepage and throughout the website.
- **Add video elements to your website** – such as a welcome video or having a video describing the different appliance repair services that you offer.
- **Showcase your online reviews more prominently on the homepage** – You can use sites like birdeye.com or reviewbuzz.com.
- Get the basics in order, such as the **phone number in the upper right**-hand corner of your website.
- Have a **web form**
- Use **authority symbols** like the Better Business Bureau and Angie's list.
- Have **call to actions** throughout your websites – Let consumers know what you want them to do.

Chapter 13 - How Much Your Leads Are Really Worth?

In this next chapter, I want to discuss what a lead our customer is worth to your appliance repair company, this is one of the most important chapters in this book because without knowing this number, you are blindly advertising.

Today I want to discuss with you the lifetime value of what a customer is actually worth to your appliance repair business.

You already have a good idea about how much the average consumer spends for a service call fee, as well as the average repair job and I know for the repair costs that can vary depending on the type of appliance, the brand of the appliance and also the problem with the appliance, but that is why we are going to just focus on averages in today's email.

Most appliance repair companies only focus on gaining new customers and do very little to nurture the relationships with their existing customer base, mainly because they believe if they do a good job, then the customer will just call them back, but more times than none and I'm sure you will agree, this is not always the case.

At The Appliance Experts we track everything we can, including phone calls, which comes through a call tracking number, so we see it all the time where 6 months or more will go by, and the same customer is calling back as if it was the first time they found one of our ads and the only reason they called back through our advertising is because of our premium ad position across several advertising platforms.

According to HBR or the Harvard Business Review, it is 5 times more expensive to gain a new customer than it is to keep one of your existing customers. So, whatever you are paying for appliance repair leads right now, just divide that by 5 to get an idea of what the cost is to retain your existing customers.

Big savings!...right??

Now the cost of getting a new lead is important, but it's not the only thing you should be focused on, which is why we are discussing Lifetime Value today. You also have to factor in the customer calling in again for a repair on other appliances within the same year and getting referrals from them. With the right follow up with your new leads you can directly affect the amount of repeat and referral business your company gets, as you will be the first thing that comes to mind when your existing customer base ever needs an appliance repaired, as well as if any of their friends and family need to get an appliance fixed.

You are only paying for the new lead once.... well you should be, if you are paying for repeat leads, it may be time to look into a new appliance repair lead generation provider, as that will be hurting your R.O.I big time!

At The Appliance Experts, we have a proprietary lead generation software that keeps track of repeat leads so that you do not get charged for the same lead multiple times.

Ok, so you may be saying yeah, even if I only pay for the leads once, there is a cost associated with following up.... And you are absolutely right, but it's minimal when compared to the cost's of getting a new lead, and I can show you ways to automate a lot of that follow up, like doing email marketing.

As an owner or manager of an appliance repair company, you can't ignore the fact that a consumer can bring in additional revenue to your company long after the initial repair, such as:

- Referring their friends and family – because they now trust you.
- Getting another appliance fixed

- Buying additional services – maintenance contracts or annual inspections.

Every single lead can and should represent more than one revenue stream for your business and now let's take a look at calculating the Lifetime Value Of A Customer for your local appliance repair company.

	A	B
1	**Lifetime Customer Value Calculation**	
2		
3	Avg. Repair Per Customer	$150.00
4		
5	Number of Visits Per Year	x 2 visits
6		
7	Avg. Years As Customer	x 5 years
8		
9	Maintenance Contracts (optional)	
10		
11	**Lifetime Customer Sales**	$1,500.00
12		
13	Total Customer Referrals (2 referrals x $1500)	$3,000.00
14		
15	**Total Lifetime Customer Sales**	$4,500.00
16		
17	Gross Profit Margin	x 30%
18		
19	Lifetime Customer Value	$1,350.00

What does your Lifetime Customer Value look like?

Go ahead and swap out some of those numbers if they don't match up with the actual numbers of your particular appliance repair company so you can figure out your LCV.

If you are aware of how much each or your appliance repair customers are worth, you will quickly see the importance of how this can help you make critical decisions when it comes to your appliance repair lead generation, marketing, and advertising, as it directly impacts the way you retain existing customers and acquire new ones.

So now that you know the Lifetime Value of your customers, what will you start to tweak with your marketing, advertising or lead generation?

Action Items:
- Calculate the Life Time Customer Value for your appliance repair company.
- Create an incentive program to get more recommendations and referrals from your existing customers.
- Offer rewards for customer loyalty.
- Create plans to increase repeat business.
- Determine which source of advertising and marketing to focus your lead generation budget on, that are the most cost effective and that drives the highest Return On Investment.
- Figure out how much to actually spend to get a new appliance service customer.

Chapter 14 - Do You know the "True" cost of your leads?

What we are about to discuss, is an insider secret that the big appliance repair lead generation providers don't want owners of appliance repair companies to find out, as they may and will start losing customers and market share.

Let's start with Google AdWords, maybe you have tried it yourself, and you realized that it was just costing you a fortune, as it seems like you were only paying for clicks. So instead of giving up and just moving on, you decided to hire a company to manage your account for you. Sure, you will have to pay $500-$2500, and a percentage of your ad spend to them, but at least they will do a better job and actually get you some customers.

If you were to ask your account manager what it is costing you per lead, they might tell you something like $5-$20 per lead, but what they are actually telling you is what it's costing you per click. So, they will look back into your account and see which click actually turned into a phone call to your appliance repair business and give you the cost of that particular click.

But is that really the TRUE cost of your leads???

Probably not, now that all account managers will try to mislead you to keep you as a client, but it's important that if you run an appliance repair business that you know how to figure out the true cost of your leads, whether you have an account manager, an employee or if you are doing your Adwords account management yourself.

	A	B
1	How Much Did You Pay Google Adwords This Month	$500.00
2	Average Cost Per Click ($5 -$30)	$10.00
3	How Many Clicks Did You Get This Month	50 Clicks
4	How Many Clicks To Get A Call (Avg 4-8 Clicks)	4 Clicks
5	How Many Leads Did You Actually Get (Not Clicks)	12
6	Management Fee ($500-$2500)	$500.00
7	Total Cost	$1,000.00
8	**Actual Cost Per Lead**	$83.00

In the above example, I used the number on the low end, but take some time now and go ahead and plug in your actual numbers, you may be surprised by what it's really costing you to get a customer to call your appliance repair business.

Now if for some reason you are not tracking your calls, you may not be able to figure out how many clicks are converting into calls and now would be a good time to start implementing conversion tracking within Google AdWords, it's relatively easy to set up.

Now what if you are not using Google AdWords to get leads, but instead you are buying leads from a lead generation company, it's still important to know your numbers so you can figure out the true cost of your leads.

Let's say you are buying shared appliance repair leads for $12 if you were to get 10 leads today, how many of those are you actually converting into a customer?

Most of the appliance repair companies I speak to will say 30% unless they are in an area where there are only few appliance service companies using the same lead generation company, then you will have higher conversions.

Now you can also have higher conversion rates if you are the first to contact the lead once you receive the alert from the lead generation company, but even then, because they send the same lead to multiple of your competitors, you never know if when your competitor calls the lead if they will offer a lower service call fee or if they can get out to the customer sooner or at a time more convenient to them and as a result they win the lead.

So, let's look at the formula to calculate the true cost of your leads from the lead generation company, and you can plug in your actual numbers to see if the leads make sense for your appliance repair company:

	A	B
1		
2	Cost Of 10 Leads	$120.00
3		
4	30% Conversion Rate	3 Leads
5		
6	**Actual Cost Per Lead**	$40.00

If you are at a 30% conversion rate or lower after doing the calculation, you should definitely look into improving that and that may be as simple as figuring out a way to be the first to respond to the lead alert and if your availability is a problem where you are not able to offer same day service, then you can look into options to fix that also.

You want to make sure you are doing everything within your control to improve your conversion rates, so you can reduce the amount of money you are losing.

Now most appliance repair owners tend to blame the lead source when leads don't work out as planned, and sometimes it is the lead source, as the reality is that shared lead programs benefit the lead source more than it does the actual appliance repair company, because the lead source makes a lot more money selling shared leads.

Just to be fair, before you begin pointing the finger, look within your company to see if there are things that can be improved. If after doing that you realize the conversions are still too low because of outside sources like your competitors just keep calling the leads and telling them horror stories about your company or they just keep offering lower prices, then it may be time to look into more profitable lead sources.

At The Appliance Experts, we don't believe in shared leads, as we would rather create a more win-win situation with our partners. Our long-term partners are seeing an 80-90% conversion rate with our leads, which is probably the highest in the industry.

Full disclosure: The reason they are seeing these high conversion rates is not because of the high quality of the leads, well that is part of the reason, but the other big part of that is because they have the right systems in place, such as having a dedicated person or persons answering the phones that are polite and professional, some may have an answering service and they have multiple technicians so that they can offer same day service, as well as after hours and weekend service for those consumers that can't get a day off during the weekdays.

Having the right systems in place will give you the best opportunity to close as many leads as possible.

There are several sources where you may be buying appliance leads from, but let's look at another one you may be using or considering, lead generation companies that sell phone call leads.

We have to approach this lead source a little differently and what you want to focus on here is mainly what your Return On Investment is. They provide live phone call leads, which is great because they are hot prospects, but the ROI can be low if they charge for ALL leads that are appliance repair related. That means you will pay for small appliance repair calls like blenders, toaster ovens, parts, commercial appliance repair calls even if you don't work on commercial appliances.

Another drawback with their leads is that they list your company on their directory website with up to 10 competitors or more, and while they promote their leads as exclusive, this type of directory website encourages the consumer to shop around, so while they are not intentionally sharing the leads, this type of set up will hurt your conversions.

So, if you are noticing a lot of calls where the consumers just seem to be shopping around, this is probably one of the reasons why.

And we all know who gets the majority of the leads…..the company listed at the top which is normally one of the big players, Sears or Mr. Appliance. And you can look at any city across the U.S.; you will still see these same 2 companies at the top.

Let's take a look at the math:

	A	B
1		
2	Cost Of 10 Leads	$250.00
3		
4	Number Of Qualified Leads	5
5		
6	Time It Cost To Dispute Leads	
7		
8	Actual Cost Of Lead	$50.00

These unqualified calls not only waste your time, but they also eat up your profits. Then on top of that, you need to dispute an unqualified lead, prepare to follow up with them multiple times and good luck getting a refund or account credit.

Action Items:

- Make a list of all the fees that are involved with all sources, set up fees, monthly fees, management fees etc.
- Calculate your conversation rate for all of your advertising and lead sources, such as how many clicks to get a phone call, how many leads to get a scheduled job etc.
- Calculate your "True Cost Per Lead" for all sources to see if it makes sense to continue using them and once you find the one with the best ROI, you may want to investment more there.

Chapter 15 - Do You Know Where Your Appliance Repair Leads Are Coming From?

If you are doing any type of online marketing for your appliance repair business, you must be aware of some of the tactics such as social media marketing, PPC, Search Engine Optimization, blog posting, and banner advertising.

Wouldn't you like to know which of these forms of appliance repair advertising is bringing in the maximum leads for your business?

Tracking the source of your appliance repair leads is the easiest way of determining the success of your marketing effort. If you don't have a system to track the source of your leads, then you could be wasting money.

Here are 4 ways of finding out where your leads are coming from:

Ask your Lead Directly

Conversing with your prospects is essential to build rapport with them. You can also train your employees to find out how the prospect was able to find details about your company. For instance, if a prospect calls your company for appliance repair needs, your customer support team can ask them how they came to know about your company. If you have an online form on your website, you can ask the visitors to answer how they found out about your website.

The best way of tracking the results is by putting a system in place to record the information. You can record the information in a simple spreadsheet, and the marketing team can use this information to develop their marketing strategy. The only drawback of this approach is that it is manual and must be constantly updated. If the data is not updated, it could jeopardize your marketing strategy. Also, some prospects may be influenced by several sources, so they may not articulate or remember the primary source that brought them to you.

Unique Tracking ID

A unique ID can be given to each online campaign or marketing initiative that takes people to your appliance repair website. This technique is effective for marketing tactics such as social media marketing, online advertising, and email marketing that are designed to drive clicks to your website. Then you can use Google Analytics to find out which ID's are driving the most traffic to your site. However, this method does not provide user specific details, so you may not know the actual conversion rate of the leads.

Call Tracking

This technology allows you to put a unique tracking number to your marketing sources, such as offline marketing tactics or PPC ads, which gives you an ability to see where the leads are coming from. It also gives you the option to record calls, so you get more information about your customers and appliance service leads. This method is especially useful when used with other approaches such as lead tracking software or unique tracking ID. Some call tracking providers you can look into are **www.callfire.com and www.callrail.com**.

Software to Track Leads

Since the leads can contact you in several ways, using call tracking is not sufficient. Also, tracking calls may not be ideal on a few sources such as local listing. You will need a lead tracking software to track form submissions and conversations. This software uses special codes to find the source of lead generation. Some software solutions provide additional details about lead information, site traffic, and call recordings. This will give you better information about how the leads are getting details of your business. When you use this software, you get better visibility into the effectiveness of your marketing strategy.

How Call Tracking Can Benefit Your Appliance Repair Company

One of the biggest mistakes that appliance repair companies make is not tracking the results of their advertising campaigns, so they never really know which source is actually working for them. The easiest way of keeping track of both online and offline marketing campaigns is by using call tracking. When you use call tracking, you can easily find out which campaign is driving the greatest number of appliance repair leads to your business.

What is Call Tracking?

It is a process of putting a unique phone number on an advertising campaign to measure the effectiveness of the campaign. These phone numbers are trackable, and the calls can be recorded. The recording can be used to find out how the calls were handled and whether it led to an appointment with the technician. Call tracking is an easy and a cost-effective method of tracking the source of lead. This is especially important for appliance repair companies as their business's first call to action is a simple phone call. For instance, if you place online ads, television ads, print ads or use radio spots to promote your business, you can use different call tracking numbers in each of these platforms. When you receive a phone call from the prospect, you can analyze the effectiveness of each marketing platform.

Important Metrics

Some important details that call tracking provide includes:

Number of Calls

This information can used to find out how many prospects called you after seeing a particular campaign.

Duration of the Call

Usually, long conversations are likely to increase your conversion rate because they indicate high customer interest.

Conversion Rate

When prospects call you, they may need time to decide if they want to use your service. You can use call tracking to find out when the prospect called you. This will give you can idea of the conversion rate of a particular marketing campaign.

Cost Per Lead

Call tracking will help you calculate the cost per lead. For instance, if your marketing budget is $1000 a month and you generate 100 leads a month, you spend $10 to generate a lead. This data will help you decide if you want to increase or decrease your marketing expenses.

Day and Location

Find out when and where the most conversions emerge. This will help you maximize your returns by spending on geographies and time frames that generate the best results.

Benefits of Call Tracking

Apart from providing details of the source of the appliance repair lead, call tracking offers several other benefits. These include:

Level of Customer Service

Listening to the conversation that your customer service team has with the prospect, you can understand how the customer support executive is handling phone calls. This will help you uncover issues such as failure to handle queries and improper greetings.

Sales Training

The recorded call will help you determine whether your customer support team is asking the right questions to convert the prospect into a customer. You can use the call recording to train your support team to effectively complete the task when the prospect is on the phone.

Consumer Insight

Call recordings will help you gather insight into service issues, customer trends, and in-demand services. This can be used to adjust your service offerings. Additionally, it can be used to respond to customer complaints.

Are you using call tracking numbers in your marketing? Let us know your experience, or if you have questions about call tracking let us know in the comments below.

Action Items:

- Every single customer that calls in should be asked **"How Did You Hear About Us."**
- Consider implementing call tracking to further track how your sources of advertising are working, as well as how your internal staff are doing with customer service.

APPENDICES

The Ultimate Appliance Repair
ONLINE MARKETING CHECKLIST!

- **Is your website properly optimized for the search engines?**

  - Do you have your main or multiple keywords in the title of the pages of your website? E.g., Your city appliance repair | company name
  - Do you have pages for each of your appliance repair services?
  - Do you have pages for the major appliance brands that you service?
  - Do you have unique content on each of the pages of your website?
  - Are you helping google understand your local service area?

- **Does your website rank on page one for your most important keywords like "appliance repair + your city", "your city + refrigerator repair"?**

- **Is your website optimized to convert your visitors into callers?**

  - Do you have the phone number in the upper right corner of your site?
  - Are you using original images / video? Photos of the owner, photo of your vans, photo of your team, etc.?
  - Do you have a compelling call to action after every block of text?

- **Is your website mobile friendly?**

- Are you writing new content on a regular basis, blogging and creating new inbound links back to your website?
- Have you optimized your google map listings correctly?
    - Are you on all the major online directory listings with the same company name, address & phone number?
    - How many online reviews do you have?
    - Do you have a proactive strategy for getting new online reviews every day?
- Are you active on social media?
    - Do you have your business profiles setup on Facebook, Twitter, LinkedIn, YouTube?
    - How many "likes" do you have on your Facebook Page?
    - Are you updating your social profiles on a daily basis or weekly?
- Are you leveraging e-mail marketing?
    - Do you have a database with your existing customer's email addresses?
    - Are you sending out a monthly email newsletter?
    - Are you leveraging email to get online reviews and to draw customers into your social media profiles?
- Are you taking advantage of paid online marketing opportunities?
    - Do you have an AdWords campaign? Are you strategically targeting with specific ad groups, text ads, and landing pages?

- Do you have a premium ad on Angie's List, Yelp, City Search, Yellow Pages?
- Are you taking advantage of lead generation services –HomeAdvisor, The Appliance Experts, etc?

- **Do you have the proper tracking in place to gauge your Return On Investment?**
  - Google analytics
  - Call tracking
  - CRM with tracked lead sources
  - Google webmaster tools

Download A Copy Of This Worksheet At
Https://www.appliancerepairmarketingsecrets.com/checklist-download/

All Good Things Must Come To An End…

We are at the close of this appliance repair online marketing book, and I want to encourage you to review the action items at the end of each chapter again and use the checklist on the previous pages carefully so that you can identify any areas in your marketing that have room for improvement. As you review the checklist, ask yourself these questions:

- Am I implementing all of these online marketing strategies correctly?
- Do I have a team or resources necessary to implement these on my own?

If you answered yes to these questions, then you are in the position to take full advantage of online marketing to get all the appliance repair leads you can handle.

If you answered NO, then I have something you may want to take advantage of...

How Does A FREE Strategy Session With Me Sound?

As a special thank you gift for buying this book, I want to offer you a free session to talk one on one with me where we can discuss any challenges you are having with marketing your appliance repair business...

Is there a catch???

I do have one condition; you must leave me a review for this book on Amazon. Once you do that go to the following link to schedule your appointment:

https://www.appliancerepairmarketingsecrets.com/schedule/ or call us directly at 866.561.5627

More FREE Stuff!

While saying goodbye can sometimes be hard and with this being the end of the book, it doesn't mean we have to go our separate ways, at this point you may want to take your marketing knowledge further, or maybe you learn better by watching versus reading, so if you are one of those persons, go to this link and sign up for one of my upcoming webinars on how to use online marketing to get more appliance repair jobs here:

https://www.appliancerepairmarketingsecrets.com/webinar

You can also check out our blog for more educational resources:

https://www.appliancerepairmarketingsecrets.com/blog

I hope you found value in this book and enjoyed this book as much as I did preparing it for you!

To Taking Your Appliance Repair Business To The Next Level!

Marlon

Case Study: Tristan Lapresta, owner of Florida Appliance King in Fort Lauderdale:

When I started my appliance repair company in South Florida, I was having trouble with finding customers, but then I found The Appliance Experts, a referral company that helps appliance repair companies find good leads, that they thought they would never be able to acquire on their own. They very quickly started supplying me with 5 to 10 calls per day.

Unlike other lead generation services, they were very upfront with their communication, they were honest, and they didn't charge me for leads that were not good.

I've always been wary of lead generation services as they don't usually work out the way I would like, but with The Appliance Experts that was different. Marlon, the owner of The Appliance Experts, keeps very good communication with his customers.

After a year of being in South Florida, I now have a successful appliance repair business and have also referred my brother and dad who also run an appliance repair business in South Carolina. The Appliance Experts also gets them a lot of business, and they also have a great relationship.

The Appliance Experts is the only lead generation service I am going to continue to use, and I don't know if that will ever change, because they really take care of me and keep my techs very busy.

As far as anything bad to say about The Appliance Experts, I really don't have anything bad to say; I am really happy to have started out with them when I did because I am seeing their company grow along with mine. I value this close-knit relationship I have with the Appliance Experts.

Marlon with the Appliance Experts is a really great guy, and he really goes out of his way to make sure you are satisfied and being taken care of as a customer.

Case Study: Stephan Lapresta, owner of Star Services in Charleston South Carolina.

I've owned and operated an appliance repair company for the last 11 years in the Charleston area. When I first started this company, I started to advertise in the phone book, newspaper, and other media, and what I found is they charge unreasonable rates that were expensive, regardless of how effective their advertising actually was. I would have to pay them regardless of whether or not I got a response from their advertising.

Since those media weren't effective, I then had to do work for warranty companies to help build my business, while they would send me customers to keep me busy.

Warranty companies come with their own setbacks; they expect me to do top notch work for a bottom dollar rate. Warranty companies do not pay well for the work that they expect, and there is a lot of hassle in between, dealing with a 3rd party billing system. This all changed when I met Marlon, his service is very effective, and he only charges when we get a call to our business.

If you get into business with Marlon and his service does not produce leads, which it will NOT, you wouldn't have to pay anything, because he only charges for calls, that come into your office. He is very good at what he does, and he does a good job to make sure customers find your company, if anybody searches in my area for appliance repair, he makes sure that they find my company, and he only charges for good leads, people in my area that are looking to get their appliance serviced.

What I have found with Marlon is that he is a sincere practitioner, what he tells you to expect from his service, is exactly what you get, and he addresses any concerns in an expedient manner. I've had a really good experience working with Marlon, and I can't express how much it has changed my business. This year in the last 5 months of working with him, I have made more profit than I have made all of last year because the number of retail calls that have come in to us has increased by more than 150% from last year at this time.

My slow period this year has been busy, thanks to Marlon. I stand by and value my partnership with Marlon and will continue to use his services.

If you really want to increase your retail business, I highly suggest that you let Marlon advertise for you, he will get your new customers, I guarantee it!

Case Study #4 Tom Luben, owner of Luben Services Miami Florida.

Before finding out about The Appliance Experts, I had a really hard time finding a good source that could provide me with appliance repair leads. I've tried just about everything, Google AdWords, Bing, Newspapers, Craigslist, but none of them were working out for me, they all wanted too much money, even though they delivered not enough results.

One day I was contacted by Marlon, and he even gave me a couple leads before signing up with him. After I signed up, he sends me a constant flow of phone call leads that are ready to hire me to fix their appliances and the best part is his leads are sent exclusively to me, so I don't have to worry about my competitors undercutting me.

Marlon has even gotten on phone calls with me to help me close more of these customers. Now that I have a quality lead source, I am looking to hire more technicians to expand into other areas. I highly recommend his lead generation services to anyone that owns an appliance repair company.

About the Author

Marlon Thomas is an online marketing expert who specializes in lead generation for appliance repair companies. To learn more tips on how to use online marketing to grow your appliance repair business visit www.ApplianceRepairMarketingSecrets.com

www.ingramcontent.com/pod-product-compliance
Lightning Source LLC
Chambersburg PA
CBHW030650220526
45463CB00005B/1710